# THE DERISION OF HEAVEN

**Books by Michael Whitworth**

*The Epic of God*

*Living & Longing for the Lord*

*Esau's Doom*

*Bethlehem Road*

# THE DERISION OF HEAVEN

## A GUIDE TO DANIEL

Michael Whitworth

ISBN-10: 1941972012
ISBN-13: 978-1941972014

Library of Congress Control Number: 2013946392

Published by Start2Finish Books
PO Box 680, Bowie, Texas 76230
www.start2finishbooks.com

Printed in the United States of America



Cover Design: Josh Feit, ChurchGraphics.org

For my son

**Daniel Isaac**

May the God of your fathers deliver you
from fiery flames and dens of lions.

May you walk before the God of heaven with
the wisdom and integrity of your namesake.

# CONTENTS

# FOREWORD

The exciting story of Daniel in the lions' den is a favorite of youngsters, as is the story of Daniel's friends, Shadrach, Meshach, and Abednego, when they were tossed into the fiery furnace. In each instance, the lessons are simple and clear. Whatever trouble we're in, God is powerful enough to rescue us, and God protects those who remain faithful to him in the most trying of times. That's it, really. A comforting, encouraging message that even children can understand ... at least until we read the last chapters of Daniel and encounter fantastic, mind-bending visions, along with bizarre numbers and enigmatic periods of time that leave even the most learned biblical scholars scratching their heads.

As with John's Revelation, the visual overload of figurative, apocalyptic language in Daniel's closing chapters is as seductive to would-be savants as it is mystifying to the ordinary reader. Show me a passage that's maddeningly cryptic, and I'll show you someone who is eager to reveal each and every detail of the riddle, even if there's not a chance in the world he knows what he's talking about. What does he have to lose? If no one can possibly know with full assurance what the text is specifically referring to, the intrepid interpreter can never be proven wrong, unless he foolishly dares to date events that don't come to pass. Better yet, the more daunting the mystery, the more honor is given to the one who is seen to reveal the mystery— not unlike Daniel himself, who was honored with high positions for interpreting dreams no one else could touch. Yet there is grand irony here, since not even Daniel fully understood some of the visions he passed along to us—our first clue that caution is strongly advised.

What, then, can any commentator add, either to simple stories suitable for children or to intriguing but inscrutable visions? In a word: urgency. Michael Whitworth's greatest contribution in the pages ahead is not just his careful scholarship of the Daniel text (making it refreshingly accessible to the average reader), but also his challenge to the church to see Daniel as a must-read for Christians who are now facing the imminent prospect of spiritual exile in our own homelands. When the coming persecution arrives (and it's headed our way fast!), all the wild end-times (millennial) speculation touted by popular writers and televangelists, spawned largely by the book of Daniel, will miss the point by about a thousand years! What won't miss is Whitworth's clarion message: that the apocalyptic passages in Daniel are but a dramatic exclamation point added to the simple truths already more clearly revealed in a den of lions and a fiery furnace: Whatever trouble we're in, God is powerful enough to rescue us, and God protects those who remain faithful to him in the most trying of circumstances.

We like the first part, of course: God to the rescue. It's the second part—our own faithfulness in testing times—that demands so much more. In view of the approaching danger, we would do well to read again and again the inspiring story of God's faithful servant, Daniel. The book you have in your hands tells that story as it has seldom been told before: clearly, comprehensively, and—most important of all—urgently.

— F. LaGard Smith
*Buckland, England*

# INTRODUCTION

At this very moment, Christianity in America is wrestling with an unprecedented development—we are losing influence. There is no use denying our country was founded on Judeo-Christian principles. While not all the founding fathers professed Christian orthodoxy (e.g. Jefferson denied the Resurrection), they were nonetheless God-fearers.

But Christianity's influence in America has been declining for many years. For the first time in our nation's history, we no longer form a collective majority. In October 2012, the Pew Research Center reported that a disturbing one in five Americans claim no religious affiliation whatsoever. Some might be able to finagle other statistics to make it appear as if we retain a slightly dominant coalition, but not if you define "Christian" as one who authentically confesses Jesus as Lord and whose worldview has been saturated with Scripture.

The deterioration of Christianity's influence in our culture alarms me, but I am not so much bothered by this decline as by the church's *reaction* to it. Listen closely to the lamentations: Are we upset that God is no longer honored—

Or that we are no longer a powerful majority?

Power is seductive. Power corrupts, and absolute power corrupts absolutely. Anyone has the potential to go punch-drunk on power, to become intoxicated with the thrill of being large and in charge, and

American Christians have not always been responsible stewards of power. We have not always sought and obeyed God's will. We have not always struggled faithfully to preserve his values in the world. Instead, some among us rather enjoyed being the judgmental majority, the prodigal's older brother. And as we see our power dwindle to nothing, we are terrified, willing to do almost anything necessary to preserve what little power remains for us, even if it requires waging war with the sinful, carnal weapons of the world.

The book of Daniel begins with the collapse of a dream. The incomprehensible happened about 605 B.C. when Nebuchadnezzar deported many of Jerusalem's up-and-comers 500 miles away to Babylon. The nation of Israel was humiliated, and precious articles from God's Temple were carried off as spoils of war. In the mindset of the day, this represented a huge victory for Marduk, god of Babylon, over Yahweh, the God of Israel. A few years later, all of Jerusalem *and* the Temple would be decimated by Nebuchadnezzar's war machine. "From every outward appearance the God of Israel had fared no better than his people."[1]

Irrelevancy is a crippling reality, and *fear* of irrelevancy can motivate us to compromise and do terrible things. This is the situation Israel found herself in during Daniel's life. She was no longer sovereign in her land. She no longer wielded influence in the world. She faced a very uncertain, virtually hopeless future, and her God seemed to care not a bit.

Or worse, was simply too impotent to do anything about it.

As we discover in Daniel's stories and prophecies, God was very much alive and active for the good of his people and the glory of his Name. He was still sovereign. He intended the exile of Israel to turn hearts back to heaven. But while many in Jerusalem's government sought political ways out of the crisis, four young Jews submitted to the will of God and put him first. They in turn rose to prominence in the service of a pagan king; their example proves that God is powerful enough to give his people influence

1. Robert A. Anderson, *Signs and Wonders* (Grand Rapids: Eerdmans, 1984), 3.

and relevance in the worst of circumstances.

This gives me hope as the unthinkable starts to take place in this country. I believe the American church is headed into a form of exile. Overall church attendance has been declining for several years. Few of the powerful in this country authentically confess Christian orthodoxy, and our convictions are no longer socially popular. By almost every metric, those who hold biblical views on marriage, sexual morality, gender roles, or the sanctity of every human life (to name just a few) compose a shrinking minority. Before our very eyes, religious freedoms once thought to be untouchable are now eroding. As I finished up the manuscript of this book, several alarming news stories surfaced about the IRS targeting conservative groups and the NSA tracking cell phone and Internet activity. Many are justifiably wondering how much of a "beast" the U.S. government is becoming. In the future, churches could be fined or worse for refusing membership or employment to homosexuals, and preachers could face punishment for publicly denouncing the abortion holocaust.

Castigated and flung to the margins of cultural relevancy to gather cobwebs, what are God's people to do? Look to the Bible, of course—particularly Daniel. While studying the book, I was repeatedly brought to my knees in worship before a God who is in complete control of the future and has sworn to never abandon his people. As long as God lives and reigns, his people have hope. Christians should never fear the state; the book of Daniel assures us God has numbered the days of every wicked leader who wields power irresponsibly. Rulers may array themselves against all things godly, but he who sits on heaven's throne mocks them derisively. The example of Daniel and his friends has always inspired Christians while in the furnace of affliction. When in exile, God's people find success in conviction, not compromise. We are to be polite, and we never flaunt our piety like a red sash before a raging bull, but we nonetheless endeavor to always exalt the name of the Lord at any cost. In short, the book of Daniel teaches the church how to behave while exiled in a hostile culture.

Finally, my study of Daniel also reminded me that there is something more important than relevance, influence, or power. It's walking with the Son of God in faith and obedience so that I might bring my Lord glory, that my name might be written in the Book of Life, and that I might take my "allotted place at the end of the days" (12:13).

Perhaps God, in his unparalleled wisdom, has willed that his church be exiled in order to rediscover her priorities. Perhaps our dominance in America has left us punch-drunk with power, and so we need to revisit the good news about One who was glorified in his humility (Phil 2:5–11), One who eschewed authority over all the earth and liberated us from history's greatest tyrant (Heb 2:14). In so doing, Jesus won authority over all the earth and established an eternal kingdom. As you read this guide to Daniel, I pray that you come to know the power, love, and sovereignty of God, and that you repeatedly fall on your knees to kiss his Son.

"Blessed are all who take refuge in him" (Ps 2:12).

# DANIEL Q&A

In a recent interview with myself, I asked a few questions about this guide to Daniel. I hope the answers will orient you to the book of Daniel and to this guide.

**Q:** Who wrote Daniel?

**A:** Naturally, the first guess would be Daniel. He speaks in the first person in several places (7:2, 4, 6, 28; 8:1, 15; 9:2; 10:2), and an angel told him to "seal the book" (12:4). Also, Jesus believed Daniel to be the author since he quoted him (Matt 24:15). I'm unwilling to rule out the possibility that a later editor arranged the material by inspiration, especially the book's first six chapters in which Daniel is always mentioned in the third person. Eventually, we must acknowledge God as the author since it was his Spirit who inspired someone to compose the book and arrange it in its final form (2 Tim 3:16; 2 Pet 1:21).

**Q:** When was Daniel written?

**A:** I was afraid you would ask me that. Daniel's career in Babylon dates from 605 to at least 536 B.C., the third year of Cyrus' reign (10:1). Some scholars claim the stories of Dan 1–6 took place during this period, but that there is no way someone could have predicted the events discussed in Dan 7–12. They then argue that someone pseudonymously wrote the book of Daniel during the reign of Antiochus IV (c. 175–164 B.C.) since the events of Dan 8, 11 are commonly believed to concern Antiochus. Incidentally, this view originated with the third-century A.D. pagan philosopher Porphyry. But despite scholars' claims, there are good reasons to conclude that Daniel was written earlier than the 2nd century B.C. For example, espousing a positive view of a Gentile king (cf. Dan 4) would have been unthinkable during Antiochus' reign. It would be like trying to argue that Hitler wrote *The Book of Virtues*—it doesn't fit historically.

**Q:** Did you just bring Hitler into a Bible discussion?
**A:** Yes I did. In short, I believe most (if not all) of Daniel was written in his lifetime. The best way to disprove that it was written in the 2nd century is to read it. One clue after another will appear to the objective reader.[1]

**Q:** Why do you believe Daniel was written?
**A:** I explained that in the *Introduction*.

**Q:** So if I haven't read the *Introduction* already, I need to do so?
**A:** Yes.

**Q:** What happens if I don't?
**A:** I'll tell the IRS you're a member of the Tea Party.

**Q:** Seriously?
**A:** No, but I strongly encourage you to read the *Introduction*.

**Q:** Why is it so important for me to study Daniel?
**A:** The book has powerful stories that are too often relegated to children's

1. For a survey of the date of authorship, see Gordon J. Wenham, "Daniel: the basic issues," *Them* 2 (1977): 49–52.

Sunday school, but are never considered by adults—and we're the ones who need to heed their warnings and take comfort in their hope! The second half of Daniel may be the most misunderstood and seldom-read part of the OT. But just because a portion of Scripture is enigmatic or obscure doesn't mean it's not applicable. Just the opposite—the last six chapters of Daniel are profoundly relevant for the American church, or the church in any age for that matter. The book of Daniel is about how to live in exile—in a place that's not home. Heaven is the Christian's home (Phil 3:20), and our time on earth is to be spent seeking out another city (Heb 11:10). While here, we are to lead holy lives (1 Pet 1:15), but that isn't always easy in hostile circumstances (1 Pet 4:12–19). The book of Daniel helps us live in the here-and-now while longing for our home in the hereafter.

**Q:** How did you come up with the title, *The Derision of Heaven*?

**A:** The title was inspired by the second psalm. The book of Daniel is about God being sovereign over all things, especially the unfolding of history in spite of ungodly rulers oppressing God's people. Whether it was the scourge of Nebuchadnezzar, the arrogance of Belshazzar, or the oppression of Antiochus—every king in Daniel ultimately proves no match for God. If any ruler rebels against the authority of God and his Son, King Jesus, the second psalm says he is mocked and derided by the One enthroned in heaven—hence the name.

**Q:** What would be the best way to use this guide?

**A:** I recommend a three-pass system of studying Daniel. Let's take Dan 3 as an example. It always helps to read the passage first, read other people's comments, then read the passage again. If you want to appreciate Dan 3 fully, I suggest reading 1.) the story of Dan 3, 2.) that passage's section in this guide, and 3.) the story of Dan 3 again. Reading through the passage multiple times, plus studying it in this guide, will hopefully cement it in your mind. I'd also remind the reader that the book of Daniel is not in chronological order, so an alternative way to study the book would be to do so in chronological order (i.e. Dan 1–4, 7–8, 5, 9, 6, 10–12).

**Q:** What can you tell us about how this guide came together?

**A:** As always, I wrestled with what to include vs. omit. One of my major concerns about Bible study is that one can easily get bogged down in debates and details that don't matter. Also, surveying everything scholars say isn't always helpful. But I want the reader to understand God's Word, so I tried to answer common questions that arise from the text. Don't expect me to deal with every issue, and I don't expect you to always agree with my conclusions. I do expect you to study and reflect on your own and then make an informed decision. I want this guide to resemble a friendly conversation about Daniel, albeit a one-sided one. Each chapter ends with a few "Talking Points," points of application I hope will provide good material for lessons or sermons and spark positive discussion in a class or small-group setting. In the end, I want everyone who reads this guide to have a better grasp of what Daniel is saying and, consequently, have a greater faith in the sovereignty of God. Ultimately, the reader must judge for himself whether I have succeeded.

**Q:** What is one thing you wish you had mentioned in our last Q&A?

**A:** Well, I can't pick just one—how about two? First, I'd encourage readers to read the footnotes. Sometimes, they are only source citations. But others are filled with quotes that drive the point home effectively. Second, in my previous book, *The Epic of God,* there were several abbreviations. A few readers wrote me, asking, "What does 'ANE' mean?" There was an Abbreviations page in the back, but I should have mentioned it in the Q&A so that readers would know about it from the beginning. Then again, if the interviewer had asked better questions...

Q: Hey, uh-uh, no sir! Don't even go there!

A: Sorry.

Q: Do you recommend a specific Bible translation?

A: Not really. This guide primarily uses the English Standard Version (ESV), but it always helps to read the Bible in more than one translation, and I definitely recommend a good Study Bible.

Q: Would you like to add anything else before we wrap up?

A: Only that this book, though it is about Daniel, really has God as the hero of the story. We are thus encouraged to place a greater faith in God as the only One who controls the future and knows it perfectly. The book of Daniel inspires us to live holy, righteous lives before God so as to bring him glory. If we are in Christ, then we are members of his eternal kingdom, and not even Satan's worst should make us afraid. I want readers to rest and rejoice in that reality, and I pray it is the main thing they take away from studying Daniel.

The kings of the earth set themselves, and the rulers take counsel together, against the LORD and against his Anointed … He who sits in the heavens laughs; the Lord holds them in derision.

PSALM 2:2–4

# 1

# AGAINST THE CURRENT

I will always remember the nightmare of 9/11. If you lived through that darkest of days, I imagine you will never forget it either. I was a high school senior visiting my best friend at the time; we were playing baseball on his N64 before the day's activities. His mom came into the den and told us to switch over to the news—something terrible had happened in New York City. Over the next few hours, we were both spellbound and heartbroken. No foreign power had attacked the continental U.S. in nearly 200 years. Yet I, and hundreds of millions around the world, watched as the Twin Towers collapsed and Manhattan became a war zone. Overnight, almost every major city discovered some reason or another to fear a terrorist attack, and the subsequent anthrax scare didn't help matters.

Like many others, I had been raised to believe America was untouchable to her foreign enemies. Before 9/11, an American had no reasonable fear of invasion like someone living in parts of Europe, Africa, or Asia. But Osama bin Laden convinced us on that dark day that the world's largest superpower was profoundly vulnerable to nineteen men with box cutters and rudimentary flight skills. For the first time, my generation learned the definition of a national disaster.

The story of Daniel begins under similar circumstances. The nation of Israel was nowhere near the world superpower America was on 9/11, but what happened to her was just as unthinkable to her citizens—

Goldingay says Jerusalem's destruction was "potentially as devastating for Judah's self-understanding as it was for its bricks and mortar."[1] Whenever God's prophets had warned that Babylon would bring disaster on the holy city, such a scenario had been unbelievable. The people taunted and derided those men who dared repeat Yahweh's warning. Jeremiah complained, "You pushed me into this, GOD... And now I'm a public joke. They all poke fun at me" (Jer 20:7 Msg). On another occasion, and just a few years before the events of Dan 1:1–2, Jeremiah was almost executed for his "treasonous" preaching (Jer 26:1–24).

The Israelites disregarded the prophetic warning because they could not bring themselves to believe that God would allow his Temple and throne to be destroyed (cf. Jer 7:4; 14:21).[2] Was he not protective of his dwelling place (cf. Ps 132:14)? Had he not relented and preserved the city in the days of Hezekiah (2 Kgs 19:32–35)? Would he not honor his covenant with David (2 Sam 7:16)? Though he was God's spokesman, I can appreciate why Jeremiah's preaching was considered by some to be both treasonous and blasphemous. Old Testament historian John Bright concludes, "Elevated by theological optimism, the nation marched toward tragedy confident that the God who frustrated Sennacherib would frustrate Nebuchadnezzar also."[3]

But disaster, not deliverance, awaited Israel.

Disaster can undermine faith in God, but so can disorientation. Daniel and his three friends were uprooted and transported to an exotic metropolis 500 miles away from home to serve in the king's court. Given their young age and immersion into a pagan, libertine culture, conditions were ripe for these young men to jettison the values of their godly upbringing. Where had devotion to God gotten them, after all? Like disaster, disorientation can lead to spiritual rebellion—both can become

1. John E. Goldingay, *Daniel* (Dallas: Word, 1998), 21.

2. "Where is God, if he does not defend his own temple?" (John Calvin, *Commentaries on the Book of the Prophet Daniel*, trans. Thomas Myers [Grand Rapids: Eerdmans, 1948], 1:86).

3. John Bright, *A History of Israel*, 4th ed. (Louisville: Westminster John Knox, 2000), 332.

the breeding ground for disappointment with God.

"This isn't the life I wanted."

"I never dreamed this would happen."

"Why do I feel so alone?"

"I wish things would go back to the way they were."

"Why do I feel so unsure about everything?"

In these moments, we're tempted to abandon our reliance on and allegiance to God—the frustration is simply too great. But the example of Daniel shines like a brilliant lighthouse in a furious storm. Even at a young age, Daniel trusted God and knew he was in control. Instead of making things happen for himself, Daniel knew that the path to success in any set of circumstances is through resolve, not rebellion; conviction, not compromise.

Daniel thus illustrates for us how to successfully swim against the current of a culture hostile to faith and obedience. The world says that, in moments of disaster and disorientation, the only one you can trust is yourself. But over the span of nearly seven decades, Daniel proved such a trust is misplaced. Our faith must be in the God of heaven who is in complete control of all things, *especially* in times of disaster and disorientation.

God always provides for those who trust in him.

## NEBUCHADNEZZAR

If for no other reason than he is a key figure in Dan 1–5 (not to mention the OT; he's named about ninety times), it will help you to know a little about Nebuchadnezzar—known formally as Nebuchadnezzar II, but simply "Chad" to his friends. His name meant "O Nabu, protect my offspring"[4]—Nabu was the son of the chief Babylonian deity Marduk (cf. Isa 46:1). Nebuchadnezzar was by far the greatest king of the Neo-Babylonian Empire, and among the greatest monarchs of antiquity.

His Chaldean father, Nabopolassar, had usurped Babylon's throne

4. D. J. Wiseman, *Nebuchadrezzar and Babylon* (Oxford: Oxford Univ. Press, 1985), 3.

in 625 B.C. and expanded the empire. Nebuchadnezzar was a formidable military commander in his own right; as the crown prince, he defeated the Egyptians at Carchemish (cf. Jer 46:2) in May–June 605, thereby opening the door to the conquest of Syria and Palestine. Nabopolassar died a few months later in Aug 605, and Nebuchadnezzar hurried back to Babylon to ascend his father's throne on Sept 7. Nebuchadnezzar reigned until his death in Oct 562, at which point his son Amel-Marduk (known in the OT as Evil-merodach) assumed the throne.

## DANIEL 1:1–2

Determining exactly when the events of 1:1–2 took place is a bit complex, but when all the pieces are assembled, this is what we have. Jehoiakim became king of Judah in 609 B.C. after his father Josiah was killed in battle at Megiddo against the Egyptians. For a mere three months, Jehoiakim's brother Jehoahaz reigned, but he was quickly deposed and carted off to Egypt by Pharaoh Neco. Jehoiakim was then installed as a puppet king (2 Kgs 23:29–35). You'll remember Jehoiakim as the fool who cut up Jeremiah's scroll with a pocketknife and tossed it into the fire (Jer 36:20–28); his popularity as king earned him an ass's funeral (Jer 22:19).

Having whipped Egypt at Carchemish, Nebuchadnezzar[5] "besieged" Jerusalem in Jehoiakim's third year and deported many of her quality young men (1:3).[6] There is an alleged contradiction with this dating since Jer 25:1 claims this event occurred in Jehoiakim's *fourth* year. But the differences can be resolved by noting that Israel and Babylon accounted the years of a king's reign differently; Israel considered a king's first year

---

5. Critics allege Nebuchadnezzar being called "king" in 1:1 is historically inaccurate, but the reference is meant to be a prolepsis, not unlike a biographer employing the phrase, "When President Washington was a child," though he wasn't president until age 57 (Edward J. Young, *The Prophecy of Daniel* [Grand Rapids: Eerdmans, 1949], 35).

6. It's possible the first deportation did not take place until Feb–Mar 604 (Mark K. Mercer, "Daniel 1:1 and Jehoiakim's Three Years of Servitude," *AUSS* 27 [1989]: 179–92). Jehoiakim was deported, but was then allowed to return to Jerusalem and become a vassal king, paying tribute for three years before revolting in 601 (cf. 2 Kgs 24:1; 2 Chr 36:6–7).

as his first year, but Babylon factored the first year as the "accession year," and the subsequent year as Year 1, etc. This explains why Jeremiah, using Israel's dating, would say it was in Jehoiakim's fourth year, while a writer in Babylon, using Babylon's dating system (e.g. Daniel), would say it happened in Jehoiakim's third.[7] Confusing, I know, but no more so than trying to keep time zones straight while traveling in a place like northern Arizona during the summer (e.g. Arizona time, Navajo time, Las Vegas time).

It is also alleged that the author of Daniel was fuzzy on history since Nebuchadnezzar did not lay siege to Jerusalem on this occasion, at least not in the typical way we think of a siege. But the Hebrew text only says he "threatened Jerusalem."[8]

That said, the point I really want to make is that it matters less *when* these events took place as opposed to *why*. This, I believe, is the real interest of the narrator. From every secular observer, Jerusalem collapsed before the onslaught of Nebuchadnezzar because she was simply the weaker opponent. But the Bible would have us confess it was because the God of Israel chose to deliver the nation into the hand of Nebuchadnezzar. He did so to discipline her for her unfaithfulness to him. In an effort to bring her to repentance, he had unsuccessfully warned her of this disaster (cf. Lev 26:27–39; Jer 20:4–5; 25:1–11), but when the people refused his gracious offer, God was forced to act, for he does not make empty threats.

One scholar asserts, "It can readily be seen that no small nation, obedient or disobedient, could have withstood the onslaught of Nebuchadnezzar's armies." This same author wonders aloud whether "an obedient Judah [would] really have thwarted the expansionist policies of Babylon?"[9] But the Bible says Jerusalem fell because of her wickedness

7. Gerhard F. Hasel, "The Book of Daniel: Evidences Relating to Persons and Chronology," *AUSS* 19 (1981): 47–49.

8. Joyce G. Baldwin, *Daniel* (Downers Grove, IL: InterVarsity Press, 1978), 78. "Besieged" in 1:1 "may suggest more threat than substance," (Andrew E. Hill, "Daniel" in *The Expositor's Bible Commentary*, rev. ed., vol. 8 [Grand Rapids: Zondervan, 2008], 46).

9. Anderson, *Signs and Wonders*, 2–3.

and rebellion (2 Chr 36:15–21). An obedient Judah would have had no reason to fear the threat of invasion (cf. Lev 26:3, 6–8). Powerful as Nebuchadnezzar's war machine might have been, the Chaldean despot would have suffered the same fate as Pharaoh, Sihon, Og, Eglon, Jabin, Nahash, Sennacherib, and countless others had his ambitions been contrary to the will of God (cf. Ps 136:17–18).[10] No, disaster fell on Judah because she was spiritually disobedient, not militarily impotent.

And lest we waver in that confession, there remains for us two subtle declarations of extraordinary faith tucked away in 1:1–2. First, notice the author invokes "the Lord" in 1:2, rather than using the covenant name *Yahweh*. Israel's God was not just their patron deity but the sovereign Creator and Master of the universe (2 Kgs 19:15); he had just as much to do with events in far-off Babylon as he did the Promised Land.

Second, God *gave* Jerusalem into the hand of the Babylonian warrior-king, and only by submission to God could Israel be restored to a bright future. In fact, the word "gave" (Hebrew *natan*) is a key one in this chapter, occurring again in 1:9, 12, 16–17. Nebuchadnezzar toted off as spoils of war "the vessels of the house of God" (1:2; cf. Isa 39:6), likely meaning the basins, censers, and bowls mentioned in Ezra 1:7–11. Nebuchadnezzar put these in "the house of his god," meaning Marduk's temple, a grand building known as *Esagila* that rose to about 300 feet.[11] The king thought his god Marduk had been victorious over Yahweh (cf. 1 Sam 5:2). But God had *given* Jerusalem to him (cf. 1 Kgs 13:26; 14:16; Isa 34:2), meaning the collapse of the holy city was proof of God's power, not evidence to the contrary. God remained sovereign.

And he was about to exercise his sovereignty for the benefit of four special servants.

---

10. "A major concern of the book [of Daniel] is to reinforce the belief that the sovereignty of God far surpasses the power of even the most mighty of human rulers," (Tremper Longman III, *Daniel* [Grand Rapids: Zondervan, 1999], 46.

11. Wiseman, *Nebuchadrezzar and Babylon*, 71.

## DANIEL 1:3–7

Here we are introduced to Daniel and his three friends. All four may have been members of the royal family (Isa 39:7) and were likely in their teens; Daniel lived throughout the entire exile (1:21; 10:1), and ancient Greek sources claim Persia began a similar three-year education at age fourteen (Plato, *Alcibiades* 1.121; Xenophon, *Cyropaedia* 1.2.8). The captives are said to have been "without blemish" (cf. 2 Sam 14:25), a term often used in Leviticus of sacrifices. This detail negates the rabbinical tradition based on Isa 39:7 that these young men were eunuchs (cf. Deut 23:1). The captives were also "of good appearance" (cf. 1 Sam 9:2; 16:18), "skillful in all wisdom," and so on.[12] In other words, these were good-looking, very smart young men who held great promise—the kind you'd want your daughter to marry.

There are likely several reasons why Nebuchadnezzar chose to deport the elite young men of a vanquished nation (not an uncommon practice), including the discouragement of rebellion and the indoctrination of future leaders of the empire.[13] They would take a few hometown boys, propagandize them with the Babylonian worldview, and then send them home to govern as puppet-leaders. Others would stay in positions of power in the palace, just as Daniel did. It wasn't just boys from Jerusalem who were taken, but also those from Egypt, Phoenicia, and Syria (Josephus, *Apion* 1.137). As part of their training, they were allowed to eat and drink from the king's table but were also subjected to a daunting academic track designed to make them thoroughly Babylonian in every conceivable way.[14]

Learning to read and write the language would have been a difficult

12. "The three phrases used of the youths' mental qualifications are simply accumulative and do not permit analysis into distinct mental functions," (James A. Montgomery, *A Critical and Exegetical Commentary on the Book of Daniel* [Edinburgh: T & T Clark, 1927], 120).

13. Goldingay, *Daniel*, 15.

14. "The Babylonian king was not content to capture the bodies of those who had been deported from Judea, he had to capture their minds as well," (D. S. Russell, *Daniel* [Philadelphia: Westminster Press, 1981], 19).

assignment for even the brightest captives, and becoming proficient in it required an immersion in Babylonian literature. Students would make copies of texts from subjects such as math, science, literature, history, and religion.[15] For a Jew, "To begin to study Babylonian literature was to enter a completely alien thought-world."[16] Put plainly, the Babylonians had a radically different worldview than the Israelites, and the differences went much deeper than those of a poly- vs. monotheistic society.

It intrigues me that the narrator does not object to Daniel and his friends being subjected to what amounted to brainwashing. Babylonian practices such as sorcery, astrology, and divination were forbidden under the Law of Moses (Deut 18:10–14). We can only assume these four young men had a strong faith in the God of Abraham and were quite capable of subjecting their newfound knowledge to the wisdom of Yahweh (cf. 2 Cor 10:5). Their example says it's possible for one to enroll in a public institution of learning that promotes ungodly values and still graduate with a faith intact (cf. John 17:14–19).[17] That point may not earn me "Outstanding Homeschool Alumnus of the Year," but I maintain the church needs leaders who have studied and understand culture so we might engage it in productive dialogue as Paul did in Athens. We also need the ability to discern truth from error when the latter threatens Christ's body.

> It may sound a paradox, but it is a deep truth that unfavourable circumstances are the most favourable for the development of Christian character. ... Remember

---

15. A. Leo Oppenheim, *Ancient Mesopotamia*, rev. ed. (Chicago: Univ. of Chicago Press, 1977), 235–49.

16. Baldwin, *Daniel*, 80.

17. Jerome says Daniel and his friends endured their pagan education, "not that they may follow it themselves, but in order to pass judgment upon it and refute it," (*Commentary on Daniel*, trans. Gleason L. Archer, Jr. [Grand Rapids: Baker, 1958], 21). I'm also fond of Robert Murray M'Cheyne's quote: "Beware of the atmosphere of the classics. ... True, we ought to know them; but only as chemists handle poisons—to discover their qualities, not to infect their blood with them," (Andrew A. Bonar, *Memoir and Remains of the Rev. Robert Murray M'Cheyne* [Edinburgh: Oliphant, 1864], 39).

> Daniel, in that godless court reeking with lust and cruelty, and learn that purity and holiness and communion with God do not depend on environment, but upon the inmost will of the man.[18]

Consistent with a very common practice of antiquity (cf. Gen 41:45; 2 Kgs 23:34; 24:17), the names of these four young men were changed, and it "involved the idea that the god of those who bestowed the new name was to be honored rather than the god of the vanquished."[19] "Daniel," meaning "God is my judge," became "Belteshazzar," meaning "Bel, protect his life!" "Hananiah" ("Yahweh is gracious") became "Shadrach" ("Command of Aku"); "Mishael" ("Who is like God?") became "Meshach" ("Who is like Aku?"); "Azariah" ("Yahweh has helped") became "Abednego" ("servant of Nego/Nebo," a variant of "Nabu").

## DANIEL 1:8–21

At the very heart of this story is Daniel's resolve not to eat the food or drink the wine of the king's table. To appreciate Daniel's commitment, we must determine what was at stake—why did Daniel consider this food and wine to be defiling?

***The food and wine had been sacrificed to idols.*** This was a well-attested practice in antiquity (e.g. Exod 34:15; Deut 32:38; Acts 15:20; Rev 2:14), and it's understandable how it would have created a conflict of conscience for anyone intent on honoring God.[20] This very tension lies behind Paul's comments in Rom 14 and 1 Cor 8, 10. But notice Daniel did not refuse to eat *all* the food from the king's table, only the meat. The

18. Alexander Maclaren, *Expositions of Holy Scripture: Ezekiel, Daniel, and the Minor Prophets* (Grand Rapids: Eerdmans, 1938), 69–70.

19. H. C. Leupold, *Exposition of Daniel* (Grand Rapids: Baker, 1949), 64–65.

20. The same Greek word used for "defiled" in the LXX of 1:8 is also used in Acts 15:20, where food offered to idols may also be in view.

vegetables he requested (1:12) would have been offered to idols also.[21]

***The food was not kosher.*** There was a legitimate concern in the exilic and post-exilic period with eating food forbidden by the dietary laws of Leviticus (cf. Ezek 4:14; 1 Macc 1:62–63). But if this was the case with Daniel, why was he also conscientious of wine, something the Law of Moses did not prohibit? Additionally, we later find Daniel abstaining from meat and wine (10:3), but only temporarily as part of a three-week fast.

As you can see, neither of these options is a clear winner, and we become further confused when we try to understand why Babylonian names and education did not bother these four young men, but eating the king's food did. I believe a third option exists. The term translated "food" (1:5, 8) is a Persian word "meaning honorific gifts from the royal table,"[22] and accepting these gifts "implied loyalty to the donor."[23] Daniel and his friends may have not wanted to become obligated to Nebuchadnezzar anymore than necessary. Refusing the king's food gave God the opportunity to exalt them in his own way. The defilement Daniel wanted to avoid was the acknowledgment of Nebuchadnezzar as the giver of good gifts and a grand future. Daniel knew that both really rested in God's hands, so he drew a line in the sand to literally live on more than bread alone (Deut 8:3; Matt 4:4).

The word "resolved" (Hebrew *sim*) in 1:8 is among the most important in the entire book. It marks Daniel as a man of great integrity and conviction, one absolutely committed to doing God's will and bringing God glory. Anderson calls Daniel's resolve an "outward sign of a determined loyalty."[24] In a technical sense, the term means "mentally focusing on the object or issue in question, paying careful attention to it

---

21. In the apocryphal *Bel and the Dragon*, flour was offered to Babylon's false gods, and this would have been among the "vegetables" Daniel requested (1:12), a Hebrew word simply meaning any "plant raised from seed" (HALOT 1:281; cf. Isa 61:11).

22. Baldwin, *Daniel* 81. Young translates the word as "assignment" (*Daniel*, 42).

23. Wiseman, *Nebuchadrezzar and Babylon*, 83.

24. Anderson, *Signs and Wonders*, 6.

or considering its importance."[25] Used negatively, the word can represent a determined stubbornness, one that had led to the disaster now facing Daniel's people. "They made [*sim*] their hearts as hard as flint and would not listen to the law or to the words that the LORD Almighty had sent by his Spirit through the earlier prophets. So the LORD Almighty was very angry" (Zech 7:12 NIV).

In short, Daniel was doing what Israel had done (or failed to do, depending upon your perspective). Her stubborn resolve *against* God and the Law had brought disaster upon the nation. Daniel resolved to be on God's side regardless of the cost—to obey his will and seek his glory (cf. Phil 1:20). Becoming people of integrity sometimes requires us to buck the trends of so many generations before us if it means trusting God to be the true source of blessing and prosperity. Daniel proves that success in a hostile world is only found in putting God first (Matt 6:33).

Daniel's request was received semi-favorably because "God had caused the official to show favor and compassion" on him (1:9 NIV; cf. 1 Kgs 8:50; Ps 106:46).[26] God does not operate *quid pro quo*; Daniel's faithfulness did not earn him special treatment. But it is nonetheless noteworthy that God mercifully orchestrated it so that Daniel's request was well received. The official explained his reluctance to accommodate Daniel's request since, if things went poorly, it would be off with the official's head (1:10)! But Daniel spoke to the steward and arranged for only vegetables and water to be served for "ten days."[27]

Sure enough, Daniel and his friends were in superior condition due to God's blessing.[28] Not only did God grant them physical blessings, but

25. NIDOTTE 3:1238

26. "If ever under pressing circumstances holy men are loved by unbelievers, it is a matter of the mercy of God, not of the goodness of perverted men," (Jerome, *Daniel*, 22).

27. "The 'ten' days of the test is probably just a round number, not a symbolic one," (Ernest C. Lucas, *Daniel* [Downers Grove, IL: InterVarsity Press, 2002], 55); cf. Gen 31:7; Num 14:22; Neh 4:12; Job 19:3; Amos 5:3; Zech 8:23.

28. Use of this passage to promote divine sanction of a vegetarian diet misses the point.

also superior mental faculties (cf. Jas 1:17), specifically the discerning ability "to accept what was true and to reject what was false in their instruction."[29] Daniel was particularly given skill at understanding dreams, a detail prominently featured in subsequent stories. When Nebuchadnezzar inspected them, he found them "ten times better than" (i.e. head and shoulders above) the rest of the royal Magi. A God who was seemingly impotent at the beginning of the narrative when his Temple treasures were hauled away, now promoted four teenage boys above the most trusted advisors to Babylon's mighty monarch.

God hadn't been defeated at all!

Finally, the statement that Daniel served in the palace until Cyrus' reign (1:21) is more than a historical footnote. Rather, it testifies to Daniel's "staying power."[30] By God's grace, wise Daniel was able to successfully navigate turbulent political waters for nearly seven decades! Whether in times of disaster or disorientation, we can navigate turbulent waters, not by being the strongest, savviest, or most obnoxious, but by being faithful to God and bringing him glory as Daniel did.

"Remember the LORD in all you do, and he will give you success" (Prov 3:6 NCV).

---

God's grace, not vegetables, was responsible for Daniel's superior appearance—and this from the same God who declared all foods clean (Mark 7:19; cf. Gen 9:3; Acts 10:15).

29. Young, *Daniel*, 49.

30. Ronald S. Wallace, *The Lord Is King* (Downers Grove, IL: InterVarsity Press, 1979), 48.

## TALKING POINTS

THE REFRAIN OF "God gave" in Dan 1 signals arguably the most important truth for Christians: the Lord is in complete control. This is not only the overarching theme of Daniel, but it should be life's chief orienting principle. Our ability to withstand persecution, to endure suffering, or to overcome temptation depends on whether we have knelt before God's throne and said, "Not my will, but yours, be done" (Luke 22:42). We do not submit to God's sovereignty expecting him to bail us out of trouble, for that isn't submission at all. But God *has* promised to exalt those who humble themselves before him, and he does so "in due time" (1 Pet 5:6; cf. 1 Sam 2:30). Embracing God's timing as always perfect relieves us of the unnecessary burden of attempting to manage things outside our control (1 Pet 5:7). As a very young man in a foreign land, Daniel had every reason to panic, but he trusted God's sovereignty, even when the situation appeared to dictate otherwise. He knew the same God who had given Jerusalem over to destruction could likewise give him success in hostile circumstances. In the same way, the wise response to disaster or disorientation is to kneel before God's throne, confess him as "Lord," and seek to honor him in all things. That is the very definition of what it means to live by faith. Daniel's faith was rewarded, and so will ours—if not in this life, then most assuredly in the one to come (Matt 19:29)!

I'M NOT AN EXPERT ON parenting, but as a minister, I'm concerned when parents allow (or even force) their kids to pursue academics at the expense of faith in Christ, "in whom are hidden all the treasures of wisdom and knowledge" (Col 2:3). Homework is important, but not more so than the assembly of God's people, and extra-curricular activities can quickly squeeze God out of the picture entirely. Don't kid yourself: knowledge can become a god, while the fear of Yahweh is both the beginning of wisdom (Prov 1:7) and the whole of man (Eccl 12:13). Paul, whose intellect would shame many a tenured professor, warned of foolish intellectual debates (1 Tim 6:4; 2 Tim 2:23; Tit 3:9) and denounced any argument or opinion opposed to the knowledge of God (2 Cor 10:5). It's not wrong to want our kids to succeed, but parents who think grades and test scores are the sure ticket to "the good life" are mistaken. Countless college students are graduating at the top of their class, but they can't land jobs in the present economy. I should also point out it's impossible to completely shield our children from cultural brainwashing, meaning it's all the more crucial we "tell the next generation the praiseworthy deeds of the LORD, his power, and the wonders he has done" (Ps 78:4 NIV). God sent countless prophets to call his people back to faithfulness, and Daniel (directly or indirectly) benefited from their preaching. He subjected all things to the Lord and rose to prominence in the king's service, not by being the most intelligent, but by putting God first. On those who trust him, God pours out innumerable blessings—including wisdom (Jas 1:5, 17)—and gives success in the most hostile of circumstances.

IT'S IMPORTANT TO TAKE a stand and show resolve when necessary, but it's just as critical that we have the right attitude when doing so. Daniel was not rude, insulting, or "holier than thou." His request to abstain was respectful, and he was willing to seek a solution that satisfied both sides. "He never yields in devotion to principle, but he does not permit devotion to principle to serve as a cloak for rudeness or fanaticism."[31] Being a light in the darkness doesn't require our being a burr under the saddle. Over a century ago, Maclaren observed, "Many people seem to think that heroism is shown by rudeness,"[32] but Daniel modeled a different attitude, one of kindness *and* conviction, and he was successful (Prov 22:11). Paul, too, warned that a strong faith and a martyr's spirit not tempered by love are both worthless (1 Cor 13:2–3); we must treat everyone, even our ideological enemies, as precious souls created in God's image. We

31. Young, *Daniel*, 44.

32. Maclaren, *Expositions*, 42.

are called to live peacefully with everyone if at all possible (Rom 12:18; cf. Heb 12:14). Without qualities such as love, peace, kindness, and gentleness, the Spirit's fruit in our lives is incomplete. It is important that, as we stand for truth, we also check our attitudes and motives. Are we truly seeking to exalt God's principles—or our own glory?

# 2

# THE KNOW-IT-ALL

The name Youree Dell Harris probably means nothing to you. But if I mentioned her infomercial alias, "Miss Cleo," odds are the name would jog your memory—especially if you watched a lot of TV from 1997 to 2003. During those years, Miss Cleo advertised for the Psychic Readers Network and urged us (in a convincing Jamaican accent I later learned was fake) to call in for your free tarot card reading.[1]

Psychics, palm readers, and tarot card readers are the modern equivalents of diviners, magicians, and astrologers who served in the royal courts of antiquity. They would (claim to) discern the future through various means, including monitoring the night sky and investigating animal entrails (Isa 47:13; Ezek 21:21). But when Nebuchadnezzar was disturbed by a strange dream, none of his ancient psychics or wizards could help him.

All of us wish we could know something about the future. Admit it: if I could legitimately predict for you one detail about the future, wouldn't you be the least bit curious? What detail would it be?

How much longer you'd live?

Who you'd marry?

Your kids' future?

Which stocks to invest in?

1. As of late, media reports claim that Miss Cleo has appeared in commercials for a Miami-area dealership called "Uncle Mel's Used Cars." Seems about right.

Next year's Super Bowl or World Series champion?

The next Kentucky Derby winner?

The frustrating reality is none of us can predict the future, and James slaps us in the face with that cold, hard fact (Jas 4:14–15). It is popularly said by Christians, "I don't know what the future holds, but I know who holds the future." Truer words don't exist. The God of Daniel, the God of heaven, has perfect knowledge of the future. This is the clear and consistent claim of Scripture, and it is the claim of this story in Dan 2.

The belief that the future unfolds independent of heaven is without biblical basis. Rather, God has a plan, and he shapes events to ensure his plan unfolds perfectly. Nothing ever happens that God does not anticipate. Nothing can hijack his purposes. Such a fact can be both disconcerting and comforting. Disconcerting because it will sometimes prompt us to ask why an omniscient, omnibenevolent God could allow bad things to happen; comforting because faith prompts us to profess that he will allow nothing to happen unless it's for our good and his glory.

Whenever this chapter is discussed, much is said about the coming of God's kingdom. Rightly so, given the mention of the great stone and the eternal kingdom (2:44). But these details are merely alluded to; they aren't granted greater attention until Dan 7, and we will have more to say about the church there. In Dan 2, however, the text is less concerned with identifying each part of the statue and more concerned with exalting God as the only One with knowledge of and control over the future. The Aramaic terms translated "interpretation," "mystery," and "reveal" appear 13x, 8x, and 7x respectively in this chapter. In other words, this passage mentions the future advent of God's kingdom, but it is primarily concerned with God as the fount of all wisdom and understanding, even of things that remain hidden (e.g. the future).

This truth drives the apocalyptic portions of Scripture. Our apprehension and anxiety over what will happen tomorrow, next year, or at "The End" must give way to an abiding faith in Jesus and a hope in the providence of God. We may think that what we don't know will kill us, but if we serve the Lord and trust him completely, we have nothing to fear.

God knows the future.

God is in control.

## DANIEL 2:1–16

The events of this chapter took place during Nebuchadnezzar's second year (603–602 B.C.), a detail that appears inconsistent with the events of the previous chapter. How could Daniel already be in the employ of the king when he had not yet finished his three years of training? One suggestion is that Daniel and his friends had not finished their training, but were already considered part of the wise men fraternity. In other words, this story takes place *during* their training.[2] It would explain why Daniel was not present with the other wise men earlier in the chapter, and also why he had to be introduced to Nebuchadnezzar (2:25). "The denouements in 1:18–20 and 2:45–49 might then refer to the same events."[3]

The other option is to recall the Babylonian method of counting years of a king's reign, the method discussed in the previous chapter. Young argues that Nebuchadnezzar's second year was actually his third if you count his accession year—which the Babylonians didn't. He also suggests Daniel's three years may have been one whole year and parts of two others (cf. Jesus' days in the grave). Young provides this table to clarify his proposal:

| *Years of Training* | | *Nebuchadnezzar* |
|---|---|---|
| First Year | = | Year of Accession. |
| Second Year | = | First Year. |
| Third Year | = | Second Year (in which dream occurred).[4] |

2. Leon Wood, *A Commentary on Daniel* (Grand Rapids: Zondervan, 1973), 48–50.

3. Goldingay, *Daniel*, 45.

4. Young, *Daniel*, 56. Miller makes it plainer by pointing out that Nebuchadnezzar's second year would have ended in mid-April 602, while Daniel would have been deported nearly three years prior in Summer 605 (*Daniel* [Nashville: Broadman, 1994], 77).

I consider both Wood's and Young's suggestions to be equally plausible, but I also concede, along with Hill, that "a definitive answer to the chronological conundrum remains elusive."[5] What is important to note is Daniel "was not the old prophet with the long white beard that most people imagine when reading this story."[6] As suggested in the last chapter, Daniel and his friends were likely about seventeen at the end of their training, so the maturity Daniel modeled in this story is remarkable.

Was there something going on in Nebuchadnezzar's reign that caused this dream to strike such a nerve with him? The text says he was "troubled" (2:1), the same Hebrew word used in Gen 41:8 of Pharaoh being troubled over his dream. In Nebuchadnezzar's first official year (604–603 B.C.), he paraded his army throughout Syria on various military expeditions, including the sacking of Ashkelon in Feb 603. The following year, he assembled a large force and several siege weapons, and likely ventured on another campaign to Syria.[7] Based on these details, Baldwin concludes Nebuchadnezzar was overcompensating for "a fear of inadequacy."[8]

It was very common in the ancient Near East (ANE) for kings to have dreams. You will recall it was in a dream that Pharaoh was warned of a seven-year famine (Gen 41:1–8), and that Solomon received from God the gift of wisdom, along with other blessings (1 Kgs 3:5–14). Secularly, the Greek historian Herodotus recounted various dreams of Persian rulers that required interpretation by the Magi: Astyages dreamed his daughter urinated so much that she flooded Asia (*Histories* 1.107), and Cambyses had a dream that his brother Smerdis had usurped the throne, so he dispatched a trusted aid to assassinate him (3.30). Xerxes consulted the Magi about a dream before going to war (7.19).

My point is that the ancient world considered dreams a very

5. Hill, "Daniel," 59.

6. Miller, *Daniel*, 77.

7. D. J. Wiseman, *Chronicles of Chaldean Kings* (London: British Museum, 1956), 28–29.

8. Baldwin, *Daniel*, 86.

common means for the gods to communicate with men.[9] Here, God was communicating with Nebuchadnezzar by means he would accept, though not completely understand. The narrator says Nebuchadnezzar brought in a varied group of impressive experts, all of whom failed to repeat the dream back to the king. He summoned "the magicians, the enchanters, the sorcerers, and the Chaldeans" (2:2); drawing a distinction between these four offices is pointless to some degree since their roles overlapped.[10] They all utilized dark magic, sorcery, divination, and astrology[11] in an attempt to interpret dreams and discern the future. It is ominous that the Law of Moses condemned these professions (cf. Exod 22:18; Deut 18:10–14).

An interesting note: beginning with the words "in Aramaic" (2:4), the text of Daniel switches from Hebrew to Aramaic until the end of Dan 7. The reason is a mystery; we are not told why, but it is commonly believed that the portions in Hebrew were of special relevance to the Jews, while the section in Aramaic applied to everyone.[12]

Baldwin argues that Nebuchadnezzar had actually forgotten the dream, which explains why he wanted his wise men to tell him the details. "According to eastern superstition it was ominous not to be able to remember a dream." She then cites an Old Babylonian Omen Text from the Berlin Museum that reads, "If a man cannot remember the dream he

9. "[Dreams] are considered warnings issued by the gods to those who observe and understand them. The gods release these 'signs' out of their concern for king, country, city, or individual," (A. Leo Oppenheim, *The Interpretation of Dreams in the Ancient Near East* [Philadelphia: American Philosophical Society, 1956], 239).

10. Goldingay, *Daniel*, 46.

11. The Babylonian astrologers spent so much time gazing at the night sky trying to discern the mysteries of the universe that they actually became pretty good at astronomy. Naburimannu, a Babylonian astrologist who lived just after Daniel, "was able to calculate the length of the year at 365 days, 6 hours, 15 minutes, 41 seconds—only 27 minutes too long!" (John C. Whitcomb, *Daniel* [Chicago: Moody, 1985], 36–37).

12. Some contend the entire book was originally composed in Aramaic, and portions were translated into Hebrew only so that the book would be accepted into the OT canon (H. L. Ginsberg, "The Composition of the Book of Daniel," *VT* 4 [1954]: 246–75). But every suggestion on this matter is speculation and nothing more.

saw (it means): his (personal) god is angry with him."[13] However, her argument seems based on the KJV's translation of 2:5—"The thing is gone from me," instead of "The word from me is firm" (ESV). A plain reading of the story implies the king had not forgotten the dream, but desired an authentic and detailed interpretation, rather than a superficial and ambiguous one. How could Nebuchadnezzar be so troubled by a dream he could not remember?

The dreamologists of Babylon had sophisticated techniques for interpreting dreams; they had developed "dream manuals" which recorded various dreams and their appropriate interpretations based on past events.[14] This is why the wise men were so adamant for the king to reveal his dreams (2:4, 7, 10–11). But such interpretations were purely subjective given the symbolic nature of dreams.

Besides, what would have prevented the wise men from giving a selfish interpretation proclaiming divine sanction for a conspiracy or coup against Nebuchadnezzar? It certainly wouldn't have been the first time such happened (e.g. 1 Kgs 22; 2 Kgs 8:8–10; 9:6–10). This is arguably why Sennacherib of Assyria once divided his diviners into separate groups "to reduce collusion among the experts, in order to obtain a reliable answer."[15] Nebuchadnezzar believed, and correctly so, that anyone posing as a dream-interpreter would be able to reveal the dream's details. The wise men were attempting delay tactics in hopes that the dream would come to pass and thus be easy to interpret.

When his wise men proved useless, the king matter-of-factly told them "Interpret my dream, or else..." The "or else" was an oath to dismember the entire group[16] and turn their homes into public porta potties (cf. 2

13. Baldwin, *Daniel*, 87–88.

14. Oppenheim, *Ancient Mesopotamia*, 222. "Such explanations would not have been reliable but would have satisfied ignorant people," (Miller, *Daniel*, 80).

15. Lucas, *Daniel*, 70–71.

16. Dismemberment would have been accomplished by tying one's arms and legs "to four powerful trees, temporarily roped together at the top. When these ropes were cut, the

Macc 1:16; 2 Kgs 10:27). If you think such a threat too extreme to be believable, know that this same Nebuchadnezzar would later have King Zedekiah blinded, but not before making him witness the execution of his own sons (2 Kgs 25:7). Darius I once made a similar threat (Ezra 6:11) and on another occasion, he slaughtered several of his Magi (Herodotus, *Histories* 3.79). Xerxes had a group of engineers beheaded because a bridge they built collapsed during a storm (*Histories* 7.35). Saul nearly exterminated the Aaronic priesthood because they had supported David (1 Sam 22:13–19). In Dan 2, death awaited the entire corps of wise men if no one could interpret the dream. But for the one who could do so, that person would receive "gifts and rewards[17] and great honor" (2:6).

The final appeal of the wise men is very revealing—arguably more so than they intended or recognized.[18] "There is not a man on earth who can meet the king's demand . . . no one can show it to the king except the gods." Indeed. And it would not be anyone on earth who would reveal the dream and its meaning, for only God in heaven can do that, and he would give it to one of his servants, a prophet (cf. Amos 3:7). Not only did the wise men unwittingly expose themselves as complete frauds, but the Holy Spirit puts the main point of the passage on their lips: God alone is the source and giver of all wisdom, knowledge, and understanding.

Nebuchadnezzar was furious and issued the execution order; his wrath may have also been fueled by his own impotence—"Here was something that belonged to a realm in which his beck and call were not given the least priority."[19]

---

victim would suddenly be torn apart into four pieces," (Gleason L. Archer, Jr., "Daniel" in *The Expositor's Bible Commentary*, vol. 7 [Grand Rapids: Zondervan, 1985], 41).

17. Miller (*Daniel*, 82) points out that "gifts" and "rewards" are singular in Aramaic, and that they may imply something specific, such as marriage to Nebuchadnezzar's daughter (cf. 1 Sam 17:25).

18. "What for the Chaldeans is an excuse is for the author a confession," (Anderson, *Signs and Wonders*, 14).

19. Wallace, *The Lord Is King*, 50.

As the guards went about rounding up the wise men for this mass (and presumably very public) execution, Daniel intervened. Note that his reply to Arioch was with "prudence and discretion." Even the village idiot would have been able to discern the tense atmosphere that must have enveloped the palace. But once all had been divulged to Daniel, he requested an audience with Nebuchadnezzar so that he might explain the dream and its meaning. Bizarrely, the king gave Daniel the time he requested in spite of denying more time to the wise men and accusing them of stalling intentionally. God was clearly at work for Nebuchadnezzar to have done this very unexpected thing.

It seems the heart of the king was in someone else's hands (Prov 21:1). God was orchestrating events, not only to preserve the lives of Daniel and his three friends, but to also preserve the lives of all the king's wise men. "The God of Israel cares for this heathen emperor and his peace of mind, cares too, even about the fate of that handful of poor, lost, so-called 'wise men' who were little more than a pack of deluded wizards."[20] God's promise to Abraham (Gen 12:3), made so many centuries ago, was once again being fulfilled.

## DANIEL 2:17–24

In the meantime, Daniel returned to his residence and implored his three friends to join him in pleading prayer (the LXX mentions they also fasted). Their belief was that, if God made known the dream and its meaning to Daniel, it would be an act of mercy from God (2:18). They knew the preservation of their lives rested on receiving this revelation. Quite literally, they prayed like their lives depended on it! "In the book of Daniel prayer is regarded with high seriousness. It is the bulwark against every assault of the enemy."[21] Prayer should be our first line of defense. When threatened by the forces of evil, shame on us if we tweet or post to

20. Ibid., 53.

21. Anderson, *Signs and Wonders*, 15.

Facebook before praying to the sovereign God of heaven.

> Whatever God can do faith can do, and whatever faith can do prayer can do when it is offered in faith. An invitation to prayer is, therefore, an invitation to omnipotence, for prayer engages the Omnipotent God and brings Him into our human affairs. Nothing is impossible to the man who prays in faith, just as nothing is impossible with God.[22]

Daniel's subsequent hymn of thanksgiving to God[23] is a beautiful one, and I believe it is foundational to the rest of the book. Daniel "blessed the God of heaven,"[24] affirming that the God of the sun, moon, and stars had done what Babylon's pagan astrologers could not. He called for praises to be given to God without end since "wisdom and power belong to Him" (2:20 HCSB). Indeed, wisdom has been God's since before the foundation of the world (cf. Prov 3:19; 8:22–31). Whenever God's people feel afflicted, oppressed, endangered, or on death's doorstep, we should remember that God is the source of all wisdom and power. Nothing can happen to his people that he has not completely thought through from beginning to end, and he is able to intervene at any time and in any way consistent with his good will.

God's absolute sovereignty over the earth is expressed in how "he changes times and seasons"—i.e. he "makes history serve his will, glory,

---

22. A. W. Tozer, *The Set of the Sail* (Camp Hill, PA: WingSpread, 1986), 33.

23. "The test of our spirituality does not lie only in the fervency of our prayers in times of crisis, but in the wholeheartedness of our worship when God acts in grace. Relief unaccompanied by worship is never an adequate response to the mercies of God," (Sinclair B. Ferguson, *Daniel* [Waco: Word, 1988], 58).

24. This designation of God seems to have been a favorite of the Jews in the exilic and post-exilic period (cf. Ezra 1:2; 6:10; 7:12, 21; Neh 1:5; 2:4). It likely expressed for them God's universal sovereignty.

and love."[25] He is also responsible for the rise and fall of kings.[26] Long ago, God raised up Pharaoh, Sihon, Og, Hadad, Rezon, Nebuchadnezzar, Cyrus, Alexander, Antiochus, Caesar, Herod, Pilate, and Nero; there is no reason to believe he does not do so even today. To pretend that our own political leaders hold office by the will of the people and not also by the will of God is to foolishly assume that these two things are mutually exclusive. They are not (cf. 1 Sam 10:24; Acts 2:23).

Finally, God gives wisdom and knowledge to his people, and he explains what is deep and hidden[27] (Ps 139:11–12; Heb 4:13). Daniel ends his prayer by again thanking God for answering the previous prayer in which he and his three friends asked to understand "the king's matter" (2:23). Only after Daniel had received what he had requested and properly thanked God for the reply, did he announce to Arioch his readiness to go before Nebuchadnezzar.

## DANIEL 2:25–30

Arioch, "in haste," did just as Daniel asked. It seems he had no desire to follow through with the king's decree. If a senseless slaughter could be avoided, Arioch was willing. Upon being asked by Nebuchadnezzar if he could tell the dream and its meaning, Daniel affirmed what the wise men had told the king previously. "No wise men, enchanters, magicians, or astrologers can show to the king the mystery that the king has asked" (2:27; cf. 2:10-11). "But there is a God in heaven who reveals mysteries" (2:28), Daniel says. This is the same statement Joseph made to Egypt's king more than a thousand years prior (Gen 41:16). Yes, there is a God in heaven who is superior to all kings and all other gods. There is a God in

25. Wallace, *The Lord Is King*, 54.

26. "Kingship, whether native or foreign, is always treated in the Scriptures with due deference; it is an institution not without divine sanction, but it was never permitted either to usurp the power of God or to contravene his laws," (Anderson, *Signs and Wonders*, 18).

27. Miller says "deep" and "hidden things" "both denote matters inaccessible to or beyond human knowledge," (*Daniel*, 87).

heaven who, in his infinite wisdom, decided to reveal to Nebuchadnezzar "what will be in latter days."[28] If we desire to know the future, to have insight into what will happen, and to understand deep and hidden things; then it is to the God of heaven that we must submit. In 2:27–28, Daniel found a respectful way of telling Nebuchadnezzar—the most powerful person in the world—that his pagan religion was a farce[29] (cf. Isa 41:21–24), and that he wasn't all that special in the first place.

Daniel was remarkably humble in his answer.[30] He was also qualified to explain the dream to the king, not because he was more talented or gifted than the king's other servants, but because he was God's chosen vessel. Such a realization humbled Daniel and prompted him to trust in the Lord even more. "Though he is weak and knows nothing, this man is nevertheless strong and knows everything because he is trusting the living God."[31] Our personal talents and abilities matter less than our humble willingness to be used by God for his glory.

## DANIEL 2:31–45

In Nebuchadnezzar's dream, he saw a great image[32]—the Aramaic word used here means a statue, not an idol. The image had inspired awe

---

28. This phrase does not signify the end of time, only a certain point in the future (Baldwin, *Daniel*, 91), i.e. "to some decisive change at a future time," (John J. Collins, *Daniel* [Minneapolis: Fortress, 1993], 161). "A survey of the fourteen instances of the Aramaic and the equivalent Hebrew phrase in the Old Testament reveals that the expression denotes the future, but the exact time in the future must be determined by the context," (Miller, *Daniel*, 90).

29. "There is an implied put-down of the Babylonian gods, who could not benefit Nebuchadnezzar in this way," (Lucas, *Daniel*, 73).

30. "One of the big dangers and temptations in Christianity today is to be infiltrated with the cult of cleverness, but Daniel carefully removed the praise from himself and placed it upon God," (Francis A. Schaeffer, *No Little People* [Downers Grove, IL: InterVarsity Press, 1974], 161).

31. Wallace, *The Lord Is King*, 54.

32. "Apparitions of gigantic figures are characteristic of ancient Near Eastern dreams," (Collins, *Daniel*, 162).

and not a little fear in the king. It was comprised of various metals,[33] each less precious but more unbreakable than the previous one—until we come to the feet, which was inherently weak since "potter's clay and iron do not bond together."[34] A stone "cut out by no human hand" (2:34; cf. 8:25; Job 34:20) shattered the statue's feet, at which point the entire thing was pulverized into smithereens and blew away without a trace (cf. Isa 41:15–16). Meanwhile, "the stone that struck the image became a great mountain and filled the whole earth" (2:35; cf. Isa 2:2; Mic 4:1).

A word of caution: most every commentator spends time identifying the various sections of the statue. But the text does not identify any part except the head of gold—and that with Nebuchadnezzar's reign, one that effectively represented the entire Neo-Babylonian Empire since he reigned for 43 of its 55 years. More than that, it was not until a half-century had passed that Daniel received his own dream of a similar nature in Dan 7. Whereas Nebuchadnezzar saw a statue of four metals representing four kingdoms, Daniel saw four beasts (the last being quite hideous) representing four kingdoms. As is the case in Dan 2, all the kingdoms in Dan 7 are difficult to identify save the first.

Of the Bible's 425 references to gold, the vast majority of them refer to its value and superiority (cf. Job 22:25; 28:15–19; Pss 19:10; 119:72, 127; Prov 3:14; 8:10; 16:16; Song 5:11, 14–15). When Jerusalem was destroyed, Jeremiah wailed that her citizens, once "worth their weight in fine gold," were now just "earthen pots" (Lam 4:2). Being the head of gold meant that Nebuchadnezzar indeed ruled a great, majestic kingdom.

But Daniel also reminded the king that his kingdom was a stewardship from God. It had been given to him by a superior, and the kingdom would be taken away and given to another. About five years after the story of

---

33. Much has been said about how Greek philosophy divided world history into four parts, each represented by a metal of declining value; it is argued that this concept lay behind this vision. But Daniel is speaking here of four kingdoms, not four periods of history (Baldwin, *Daniel*, 98).

34. Ibid., 93.

Dan 2, Jeremiah strapped an ox yoke on his shoulders and proclaimed this word from the Lord:

> Here and now I give all these lands over to my servant Nebuchadnezzar king of Babylon. I have made even the wild animals subject to him. All nations will be under him, then his son, and then his grandson. Then his country's time will be up and the tables will be turned: Babylon will be the underdog servant.
>
> Jer 27:6-7 Msg

After Nebuchadnezzar, three more kingdoms would come—one of silver (valuable, but not as much as gold), and the next of bronze. The fourth kingdom, one of iron, would be more destructive than the previous empires,[35] but it would also be partly strong and partly weak since "the fragility of dried, unfired clay offers a vivid depiction of weakness."[36] The declining "value" of each "empire" suggests the human condition is worsening over time rather than improving. During the time of the fourth kingdom, "the God of heaven will set up a kingdom that shall never be destroyed, nor shall the kingdom be left to another people. It shall break in pieces all these kingdoms and bring them to an end, and it shall stand forever" (2:44).

Until recent times, the overwhelming majority of interpreters considered these four kingdoms to be Babylon, Media-Persia, Greece, and Rome respectively. Jews[37] and Christians[38] alike consistently adopted this view. But along with the notion that the book of Daniel was written in the 2nd century B.C. (a view that gained support for the simple reason

35. "While iron is the least-valued metal in this ranking, it is superior in strength, hinting at a government lacking in religious values or cultural achievement, but ruling with an unbending will," (DBI 427).

36. Ibid., 155.

37. E.g. Josephus (*Antiquities* 10.276) and the Talmud (b. *'Abodah Zarah* 2b).

38. E.g. Jerome (*Daniel*, 31–32) and Calvin (*Daniel*, 1:172–77).

that some scholars can't conceive of predictive prophecy), it also became commonplace to identify the four kingdoms with Babylon, Media, Persia, and Greece. In fact, Hill claims, "The issue of predictive prophecy versus *ex eventu* prophecy is the fault line" between scholars.[39] In other words, if you believe Daniel was written in the 6th century B.C. and contains predictive prophecy (as I do), you are expected to believe in the Babylon/Media-Persia/Greece/Rome interpretation; if you believe Daniel was written in the 2nd century, you're expected to believe in the other scheme.

Identifying the four kingdoms will be discussed in chapter 7; for now, I believe Lucas is correct in claiming "the identification of the four kingdoms is not crucial to the message" of this chapter.[40] But one rather ambiguous aspect of the statue is how to interpret the legs of iron and feet of iron/clay. Turner argues the two legs represented the Roman republic and Roman Empire respectively; the feet of iron/clay symbolized how the senate and the emperors never actually assimilated, but rather remained in constant friction in one another (e.g. Shakespeare's "Et tu, Brute?").[41] Hailey considered the feet of iron/clay to represent Rome's failure to assimilate its subjects.[42] Others have proposed that the two legs were Rome's eastern and western divisions, but this was not a political reality until well after the establishment of the church. Montgomery denied any interpretive significance whatsoever for the legs[43] (I think the same applies to the ten toes), and since none is mentioned in the text, I'm inclined to agree with him. If they were significant in any way, we would have been told.

---

39. Hill, "Daniel," 69.

40. Lucas, *Daniel,* 77. He later adds, "All too often, readers of Dan. 2 get so caught up in trying to interpret the details of the dream that they more or less ignore the point of it. The 'mystery' it reveals is not the details of the course of events in history, but the fact that history is under the control of God and that it has a purpose which will be achieved," (Ibid., 79).

41. Rex A. Turner, Sr., *Daniel* (Montgomery: Southern Christian Univ., 1993), 54.

42. Homer Hailey, *A Commentary on Daniel* (Las Vegas: Nevada Publications, 2001), 49–50.

43. Montgomery, *Daniel,* 187.

With all the uncertainty in this chapter, we can be certain of one thing, and that is the identity of the stone. Ironically, the stone is never interpreted by Daniel, but as Augustine asked rhetorically, "Is not this rock Christ, which was cut without hands out of a mountain, from the kingdom of the Jews, without a husband's activity? Did not that stone break all the kingdoms of the world, that is, all the despotisms of idols and demons? Did not that stone grow and become a great mountain and fill the whole world?"[44]

In Psalms, God is constantly alluded to as a "rock" (e.g. 18:2; 19:14; 28:1; 42:9; 62:2; 71:3; 89:26; 92:15; 144:1), so it is no stretch to identify Jesus—God in the flesh (John 1:14) and God with us (Matt 1:23)—as that stone. The psalmist prophesied that God's Son would dash the nations to pieces (Ps 2:9) just as the stone destroyed the statue. Jesus is "the stone that the builders rejected" yet became the cornerstone, and "everyone who falls on that stone will be broken to pieces, and when it falls on anyone, it will crush him" (Luke 20:17–18). It is not insignificant that this single prophecy, one that originated in Ps 118:22 (cf. Isa 28:16), is among the most echoed in the NT (Matt 21:42; Mark 12:10; Acts 4:11; 1 Pet 2:7).

More than the stone, Jesus is the mystery God patiently waited so long to reveal. His time on earth was known as the "last days" (Heb 1:2; cf. Joel 2:28; Acts 2:17; Heb 9:26; 1 Pet 1:20). He embodies God's grand plan to "to unite all things ... in heaven and things on earth" (Eph 1:9-10). He is "the mystery hidden for ages and generations but now revealed to his saints" (Col 1:26; cf. Acts 3:24). From Nebuchadnezzar's dream, we realize that all of history was building to the coming of Christ and the establishment of the church. Now, buried deep within our hearts, Christ is our "hope of glory" (Col 1:27).

And that's something no tyrant or empire can ever strip away from us!

---

44. Augustine, *Homilies on 1 John* 1.13. Josephus ironically refused to interpret the stone, saying, "I do not think proper to relate it," (*Antiquities* 10.210).

## DANIEL 2:46–49

Nebuchadnezzar was so overwhelmed with gratitude for Daniel's service that he "worshiped Daniel" (2:46 NRSV) and summoned incense and a sacrifice. It's difficult to believe Daniel accepted this as worship from the king since he had given God the credit multiple times in the narrative—Jewish tradition goes so far as to claim he outright refused it.[45] I admit the sight of the king worshiping Daniel in one verse, and exalting Daniel's God as "God of gods and Lord of kings" in another, seems ridiculous. That's why some translations soften the language to where Nebuchadnezzar "paid homage" (ESV) or "honor" (NIV) to Daniel. The offering and incense were brought, therefore, for Daniel to use in worship to the true God.

But this outburst of praise from Nebuchadnezzar did not signal his conversion. The pagan king would not have seen anything wrong with worshiping Daniel *and* his God. "His behaviour helps us to realize that sometimes a religious experience can stimulate an impressive response at a superficial level and yet leave us untouched in the depths of our being."[46] Nebuchadnezzar had a long way to go before his heart totally submitted to the God of heaven.

The king remained true to his original promise (2:6) and rewarded Daniel greatly. He became the ruler over the entire province of Babylon and the "chief governor" (HCSB) of the wise men, yet he was stationed in the king's court—more literally, the king's "gate" (cf. Esth 2:19, 21; 3:2–3)—where he was always at the king's beck and call.[47] Daniel's three friends (who feature prominently in the subsequent narrative) were also promoted.

45. Louis Ginzberg, *The Legends of the Jews*, vol. 4 (Philadelphia: Jewish Publication Society, 1968), 328.

46. Wallace, *The Lord Is King*, 60.

47. C. L. Seow, *Daniel* (Louisville: Westminster John Knox, 2003), 49.

WHAT HOPE THE JEWS must have felt in their soul whenever they read this story! What was God thinking when he allowed Jerusalem to be destroyed? Did he have a plan in all this? Did the death of a dream mean the death of the promises of God? Had Israel been flung to the trash heap of history, doomed to eternal irrelevance? No. God still had a plan that he was working, and he chose to reveal it in this dream to Nebuchadnezzar.

Regardless of whether the four kingdoms of Dan 2 should be identified as Babylon, Media-Persia, Greece, and Rome, God used all four to usher in "the fullness of time" (cf. Gal 4:4). Because of the Babylonian exile, the Jewish synagogue was created, which Paul took advantage of to spread the gospel (e.g. Acts 9:20; 13:5, 14; 14:1; 17:1, 10; 18:4, 19). The Persians contributed a deep respect for the rule of law, and the Greeks lent their language that became the common tongue of the first-century world, further aiding the spread of the gospel. Finally, *Pax Romana* provided easy travel and Roman citizenship to Paul, which allowed him to take the gospel all the way to the capital city. After making these observations, Rex Turner concludes, "The Roman Empire unwittingly provided a cradle or protectorate for the infant church."[48]

All this came to pass by the perfect plan of God!

This gives me hope and strength to face the unknown future. Dark days may lie ahead for the church, but God has perfect knowledge of the future, and he will thus use future events, whether they are good or bad, to bring himself glory and bless his church. Though powerless as lambs, Jesus nonetheless called us to "Fear not, little flock, for it is your Father's good pleasure to give you the kingdom" (Luke 12:32). It is left to us to do good deeds and entrust ourselves "to a faithful Creator" (1 Pet 4:19)—to bring him glory by doing the work he has for us to do (John 17:4). This means it is OK to be concerned about world events, but the proper response to them is not indignation and social media rants, but appealing to God for mercy as Daniel did. Instead of believing that this decision or

---

48. Turner, *Daniel*, 52–53.

that event will hurt the church, consider it an opportunity to glorify God and expand the borders of his kingdom (cf. Acts 8:1; Jas 1:2).

God knows the future and controls it. The future may seem like the black abyss of chaos and confusion to us, but to the Lord, "even the darkness is not dark to you; the night is bright as the day" (Ps 139:12). Salvation from all that lies ahead can only be found in Christ and his eternal kingdom, the church. God will always protect his people until his purposes have been fulfilled. "I don't know what the future holds, but I know who holds the future."

Hallelujah! Hallelujah! Hallelujah!

## TALKING POINTS

In his opening comments on Dan 2, Longman says, "God's knowledge of the future is particularly important to a people in exile and under some measure of oppression, because it implies that he controls history."[49] In this is a word of caution for the church. Those who consult palm readers or the daily horoscope to discern the future are a little nutty (cf. Isa 8:19), but no more so than those who try to secure for themselves a better future through a misuse of power. That God chose to establish his eternal kingdom without human help should give us pause. If the Lord had desired to accomplish his purposes through the political process, he certainly could have done so. But instead, he opted for what the world would consider foolish (1 Cor 1:18–31). He chose to make known his power through weakness (cf. 2 Cor 12:9). When the church opts to accomplish its mission through corrupt uses of power, it betrays its charter and its King, for "God has chosen what is insignificant and despised in the world—what is viewed as nothing—to bring to nothing what is viewed as something" (1 Cor 1:28 HCSB). Nor are we excused for playing Chicken Little or screaming about our "rights" every time the faintest wind of persecution whiffs past our nostrils. God knows the future. God is in control. God has sworn never to abandon us, but will vindicate his church and work all things for his glory and our good. Any fear or panic we might feel is not from God, but Satan (2 Tim 1:7). In times of trouble, let us follow Daniel's example: trust God completely, seek his mercy, and bless his name forever and ever.

Throughout the book, Daniel models for us how to preserve faith in God in a hostile world, and a key part of his example is how he gave credit to God. When God's people declare him to be the source of wisdom, prosperity, and sustenance, we remind ourselves that he is to be

49. Longman, *Daniel*, 73.

trusted, not ignored. Giving God the credit reminds us that we are at best participants in what he did—instruments in his hand. The alternative is that we become like our pagan neighbors and believe everything depends on our ceaseless striving. A very small way in which we declare our faith and give credit to God is praying at mealtime. Whether publicly in a restaurant, or privately in our homes, such a prayer reminds us that our daily nourishment is from the Lord. He alone provisions life and success for his people. And I'm not talking about canned prayers that can be recited while half-asleep (I'm personally guilty of too many of those), but simple prayers of sincere gratitude. Praying at mealtime may be the most profound way of declaring our God-dependence. Also, if you ask God to bless the food to your bodies, the calories are cut in half by the Holy Spirit; I'm sure that's in the Bible somewhere.

Whether in newspapers or in file footage on Al Jazeera, we occasionally observe images of our enemies proclaiming "Death to America." I want to say here and now I love being an American, and for more reasons than apple pie. Anyone who thinks we are not a blessed country has never traveled abroad. But can I tell you something that might make you uncomfortable? America will not last forever. Our enemies are right—she'll die. Who will be responsible? I don't know, though the proliferation of cat memes on Facebook has to be a strong candidate! Nebuchadnezzar's vision reminds us that every kingdom rises and falls at the Lord's pleasure, even the U.S. Of the three empires that followed Babylon, none posed a threat when the events of Dan 2 took place. Persia was subject to Babylon, the Greek city-states were at war with one another, and "the city of Rome was just being founded—an insignificant little village on the banks of the Tiber."[50] Empires and superpowers rise and fall at God's will. It's this realization that causes me to be quite concerned about those Christians who seem prouder to be

50. H. A. Ironside, *Lectures on Daniel the Prophet*, 2nd ed. (Neptune, NJ: Loizeaux, 1920), 36.

an American than a member of the church, God's eternal kingdom, one that cannot be shaken (Heb 12:28). It's not a sin to be a patriot unless patriotism becomes your idol. I wonder if some Christians aren't bigger fans of the Constitution than the gospel. In everything we say and do and support—bumper stickers, email forwards, social media updates, public and private prayers, sermons, lessons, devotional talks, protests, petitions, and at the ballot box—let us make it known that our greatest source of pride is having been rescued from the domain of darkness and added to the kingdom of heaven (Col 1:13). "Let the one who boasts..." (1 Cor 1:31; 2 Cor 10:17).

# 3

## BURNIN' LOVE

When I was in the third grade, I came down with the chicken pox. My sister had contracted the disease two weeks prior, and I was positively giddy at the thought of having it myself. I even calculated the very day on which I would begin feeling puny. Sure enough, that glorious October afternoon arrived when my dad picked me up from school and took me home for what proved to be an exciting two-week vacation from school. I must say I played the part of a sickly child quite well. So well, in fact, that dad rented a movie for me to watch: the newly released *The Last of the Mohicans*, set during the French and Indian War. I was spellbound as I watched the film adaptation of Cooper's novel.

One might reasonably wonder whether a third-grader had any business watching such a gruesome movie. One particular scene especially horrified me, though I couldn't look away. Near the end of the film, the British officer Duncan Heyward gave himself up to the Mohawk tribe to be burned at the stake.

Alive.

The image of a man being burned alive, if only in a movie, haunted me. It haunts me still. I mention that story because many Christians often handle the gruesome OT stories with too much delicacy in my opinion. I'm not suggesting we present them in all their graphic nature to our kids in Bible class. But it seems that's the only place we ever talk about them.

Anderson appropriately argues, "The familiarity attained with these stories at an early age tends to insulate the mature reader from the serious nature and purpose of the stories, and leads to the adoption of the attitude that they are not really deserving of serious attention."[1] He may be on to something. We have relegated stories such as the fiery furnace and the lions' den to Sunday school, but we rarely discuss their relevance as adults.

Has it ever sunk in that, in this story, three faithful Jews were (almost) burned alive because they refused to abandon their monotheistic allegiance to God? Don't allow its happy ending to mitigate this story's revolting horror! To be burned alive was an excruciating prospect—families of the condemned often had green wood thrown on the flames so that the victim would die first of smoke inhalation before the flames could do their worst. Imagine the worst sunburn you've ever received, multiply by infinity, and you *might* be in the zip code. This story in Dan 3 is for a mature audience if there ever was one, and relegating it to children's curriculum only injects the narrative with an inappropriate innocence.

The author of Hebrews used this story in Heb 11:34 as a brief example of trust in God, but the tension of this passage must weigh heavily on our hearts if the story itself is to make any lasting impression on our faith. We cannot reasonably expect God to deliver a happy ending to every trial, tear, or terror. This story's power is not in such a promise, but in the assurance that God is always present with us in the furnace of affliction as he was with Shadrach, Meshach, and Abednego, and that he is orchestrating circumstances for our good and his glory.

## DANIEL 3:1–7

It's unknown how much time passed between the events of Dan 2 and this chapter. The LXX, based on Jer 52:29, says this event occurred in the king's 18th year, but there is no way of validating this. William Shea poses a more likely suggestion. He persuasively argues that a revolt

1. Anderson, *Signs and Wonders*, 27.

against Nebuchadnezzar took place in late 595 or early 594 B.C., and that the events of Dan 3 took place sometime the following year. Shea says Nebuchadnezzar likely intended this event to be a state-sponsored "celebration" of national unity, "a loyalty oath on the part of all of the civil servants of Babylon." Shea even believes he has found a list of the king's civil servants that includes the names Shadrach, Meshach, and Abednego![2]

Nebuchadnezzar's statue might have been inspired partly by the dream he had less than a decade prior in which he was depicted as a head of gold atop a massive statue. Thus he decided to erect one very similar. The image "of gold" was most likely gold-plated (cf. 1 Kgs 6:21–22; Isa 40:19)[3] and stood ninety feet high by nine feet wide (cf. NIV).[4] If the statue's height did not include a base of some kind (many scholars think it did), it would have been quite perverse and grotesque to behold. But the Colossus of Rhodes, built about three centuries after Nebuchadnezzar, was taller, so this statue's height wasn't that unbelievable.

Was the statue a depiction of a Babylonian god such as Marduk?[5] Or of Nebuchadnezzar?[6] Does the narrator leave it intentionally vague?[7] We can't be absolutely sure, but I believe it was of a Babylonian god.

---

2. William H. Shea, "Daniel 3: Extra-Biblical Texts and the Convocation on the Plain of Dura," *AUSS* 20 (1982): 29–52.

3. The Tabernacle's bronze (Exod 38:30) and gold altars (39:38) were only *overlaid* with bronze (27:1–2) and gold (30:3). But a solid gold statue isn't out-of-the-question; in Babylon, Herodotus claims to have beheld a statue cast from 800 talents (i.e. 22 tons) of gold (*Histories* 1.183). Jewish tradition says the statue was cast with gold taken from Jerusalem (Ginzberg, *Legends of the Jews*, 4:328).

4. In the original language, the statue's dimensions are given in cubits, not inches (e.g. ESV, NASU); a cubit was the distance between one's elbow and the tip of the middle finger—approximately eighteen inches.

5. Wiseman, *Nebuchadrezzar and Babylon*, 109.

6. "We believe that the image was the conceited expression of Nebuchadnezzar's boundless egotism," but he also concedes, "There is nothing in the text which clearly settles the questions," (James Burton Coffman, *Commentary on Daniel* [Abilene, TX: ACU Press, 1989], 50, 52).

7. Wallace, *The Lord Is King*, 64.

1. From Nebuchadnezzar's own words in 3:28, worship of a deity was somehow involved (cf. 3:12, 18).
2. If Nebuchadnezzar was effectively deifying himself, we might expect an explicit divine censure to have followed similar to the one in Dan 4 (cf. Isa 14:13–21).
3. It is sometimes argued that Assyrian kings often erected statues of themselves to be worshipped, but there is no evidence of this ever being the case during a king's lifetime, and never in ancient Babylon.[8]
4. If the statue bore Nebuchadnezzar's image, why would he not receive worship personally since he was physically present?[9] Ancient worship of kings as deity usually took the form of worship to a statue of the king when he was physically absent.

Regardless of your conclusion, don't lose sight of the point of the text: everyone present was compelled to commit idolatry, something no Torah-loving Jew would have done. Scripture is replete with declarations that Yahweh is the only God (Isa 43:10–13; 45:5–6, 18, 21–22; Jude 25). The Lord's covenant with Israel was based on their rejection of idols and acceptance of him as the only true and living God (Ps 31:6; Isa 26:3–4; Jer 17:5, 7). Idolatry was the reason Judah had been sent into exile in the first place (Isa 30:19-22; Jer 8:19; Ezek 6:1–10), and there is overwhelming evidence that it ceased to be a problem during the exilic and post-exilic periods. "God chose Babylon as a caldron to boil idolatry out of his people"[10] (Jer 1:13–19).

The story is set "on the plain of Dura," an area six miles south of Babylon where archaeologists have discovered a mound measuring 45 feet square and twenty feet high that is believed to have been the base of

8. Archer, "Daniel," 50.

9. Longman, *Daniel*, 103.

10. Turner, *Daniel*, 83.

the statue.[11] If Dura was indeed a little ways from Babylon, but still within the province, this may explain Daniel's absence from the story.[12] His duties would have kept him at the royal palace, while Shadrach, Meshach, and Abednego were administrators over the province (2:49), and thus their attendance was mandated.

At Dura, Nebuchadnezzar gathered a long list of political leaders and cabinet members to commemorate the inaugural use of his statue. Such an event was very common in ancient times[13] (cf. Num 7:10–11; 1 Kgs 8:63; Neh 12:27). The reason, as discussed previously, was a pathetic ploy to solidify power and foster unity in the kingdom in the wake of a revolt. Surely, if there is a grand ceremony in which everyone does the same thing, there will no longer be rivalry and bitterness! Fallen humanity can have a very convoluted sense of unity.

The repetition of those gathered (3:2–3) heightens the intensity; will our three heroes conform to the call to disobey the Torah's first two commandments? Surely to reject the king's decree was madness and the peer pressure too great! If Nebuchadnezzar could build so great a statue and assemble so impressive a gathering of nobles, then he could absolutely compel all of them to bow their knee. At least that's what he thought.

When the music played, all were to bow. There was not just one instrument present, but several. The royal band had an international flavor since many of the instruments originated in Greece; the instruments were horns, pipes, lyres (a cross between a harp and a guitar), trigons, harps, and bagpipes.[14] All of these details paint a picture of grand sophistication.

---

11. Wood, *Daniel*, 80.

12. Archer lists six plausible reasons why Daniel was absent ("Daniel," 55), and his absence is also a good reason to believe in a 6th-century date of authorship. If the book of Daniel were a forged document written under a pseudonym during the 2nd century, as liberal scholars claim, it wouldn't make sense for the author to omit Daniel from this narrative (Maclaren, *Expositions*, 56).

13. Montgomery, *Daniel*, 197–98.

14. Dyer prefers to identify these instruments as a "horn, double-reed pipe, lyre, harp, dulcimer, and drum" respectively (Charles H. Dyer, "The Musical Instruments in Daniel 3," *BibSac* 147 [1990], 436).

Nebuchadnezzar wasn't the type to ever do things halfway.

The penalty for not worshipping the statue was being thrown into a "burning fiery furnace." This was not as far-fetched a punishment as some pretend it to be. Previously, Nebuchadnezzar had executed two men named Zedekiah and Ahab, likely Jews, by roasting them "in the fire" (Jer 29:22). Punishment by burning was featured in the Law of Moses (Lev 20:14; 21:9) and the Code of Hammurabi (§25, 110, 157); another king named Rim-Sin, a contemporary of Hammurabi, ordered a slave to be burned alive as punishment.[15] Execution by fire was also known during the Persian and Greek empires (Herodotus, *Histories* 1.86; 4.69).

This fiery furnace was likely shaped like a beehive and made of metal. It had an opening at the top so that the men could be tossed into it, and then a door on the side (for adding fuel) with perhaps a window so that one could look in. It was certainly large enough to walk around in, as we will later see, and it could reach a temperature in excess of 1500°F.[16] It was as convenient a means of execution as it was cruel—used to smelt the metal made to construct the statue, Nebuchadnezzar likely repurposed it for destruction once its creative task was complete.

Since the alternative was too awful to contemplate, "all the peoples, nations, and languages fell down and worshiped the golden image" (3:7). This was mass political and religious conformity with the enforcement of the state (or more accurately, a tyrant). "There was total and immediate response. The king had achieved the unity he sought."[17]

## DANIEL 3:8–18

But the response wasn't as unified as it appeared. "Certain Chaldeans"—likely astrologers and wise men from the king's court, and probably still smarting over these captives from Judah having been promoted above

15. John B. Alexander, "New Light on the Fiery Furnace," *JBL* 69 (1950): 375–76.

16. Wiseman, *Nebuchadrezzar and Babylon*, 112.

17. Baldwin, *Daniel*, 103.

them—"maliciously accused the Jews." This phrase literally means "ate the pieces of," and we're intended to see it as "severe hatred and bitter language."[18] The Chaldeans reminded the king of his decree, and that his three provincial overseers were guilty of non-compliance (cf. Esth 3:8). I guess no righteous deed goes unpunished (Matt 5:11).

Nebuchadnezzar flew into a "furious rage" when he heard this.[19] He summoned the three men and, for some inexplicable reason, was willing to give them the opportunity to prove the accusation false. Special music would be played just for them, at which time they could display their loyalty to the king. Was Nebuchadnezzar fond enough of them to extend a second chance? Or was he simply reluctant to lose such valuable administrators over a "misunderstanding"?[20] We can't know. But by extending this second chance, Nebuchadnezzar provided the opportunity for a bold declaration of faith.[21] The king's statement ended with what amounted to a dare to Israel's God. "Who is the god who can rescue you from my power?" (3:15 HCSB).[22]

One has to imagine God on his throne rolling his eyes and releasing a derisive chuckle when he heard those words. I'm not the smartest theologian in the world, but I know enough to know you don't taunt God's ability to deliver his people (cf. Deut 32:39). Pharaoh and Sennacherib had made similar boasts (Exod 5:2; 2 Kgs 18:35; 19:12–13), yet the God of heaven humiliated both of them (Exod 14:28; 2 Kgs 19:35–37).

---

18. Miller, *Daniel*, 116. The verb "accused" is "a particularly graphic" term and suggests the colloquial expression, "They made mincemeat out of them!" (Russell, *Daniel*, 65).

19. Two Aramaic words are used here; together they "give the sense of 'extreme anger,'" (Miller, *Daniel*, 117).

20. Ibid., 118.

21. "This personal and immediate confrontation with the king has a clear purpose in the story. It is one thing to defy a decree in the relative obscurity of the gathered multitude; it is quite another to continue that defiance face to face with the personification of authority and the embodiment of power," (Anderson, *Signs and Wonders*, 33).

22. This question is emphatic in the original language, signifying its importance to the entire narrative (Montgomery, *Daniel*, 208).

Nebuchadnezzar had previously confessed the God of Israel as one capable of revealing mysteries (2:47), but he could not comprehend a deity mighty enough to quench the power of fire (Heb 11:34).

The reply of Shadrach, Meshach, and Abednego is among the boldest statements in Scripture. I feel attracted to it, not only for its courage and resolve, but also because of its submission and abandonment to God's sovereignty. They would *not* reconsider as the king had invited them to do, but opted to resign themselves to God's most perfect will. Nowhere in their statement did they express a belief in the afterlife, which makes martyrdom all the more sweeter and bearable. Nor did they consider the consequence of their stand as reason to reconsider.[23] "Duties are ours, events are the Lord's."[24] No, these three men stood on little else than their love for the true God. "For them the will and glory of Yahweh meant more than fame, position, or security."[25]

There is debate as to how 3:17 should be translated. One option has the three men expressing their absolute faith in God's ability to rescue them (cf. ESV, NASU, NIV); the other option does not. The NRSV reads, "If our God whom we serve is able to deliver us from the furnace of blazing fire..." I'm inclined to prefer the former reading, but one author reinterprets the NRSV, denying there is any implication of doubt in its translation. "At all costs they intend to respect the commandment against idolatry... [Their response in 3:17–18] serves only to underline the lengths to which they are prepared to go in the service of their God and in

23. "Do not judge the situation by the king's threat and by the heat of the burning fiery furnace, but by the everlasting God and the eternal life which awaits you. ... I am glad that the three holy children were not 'careful to answer,' or they might have fallen upon some crooked policy or lame excuse for compromise. What have we to do with consequences? It is ours to do the right, and leave results with the Lord. ... Do right for Christ's sake, without considering any consequences, and the consequences will be right enough. If you take care of God's cause God will take care of you," (C. H. Spurgeon, *The Metropolitan Tabernacle Pulpit*, vol. 32 [London: Passmore, 1886], 630–35).

24. Samuel Rutherford, *The Letters of Samuel Rutherford* (Edinburgh: Oliphant, 1891), 238.

25. Archer, "Daniel," 54.

the defence of their own integrity."[26]

Their declaration was indeed bold. They believed God could save them, but they never *demanded* he do so.[27] They were in complete submission to God's will. If he saves, fine; if he doesn't, fine (cf. Job 13:15). "Thereby they indicate that it will not be a matter of God's inability but rather of His sovereign will if they do perish."[28]

Shadrach, Meshach, and Abednego were resolved together to reject worship of any god but Yahweh—the God of Abraham, the Fear of Isaac, and the Mighty One of Jacob.[29] No amount of Babylonian brainwashing could keep the Shema from reverberating in their mind: "Hear, O Israel: The LORD our God, the LORD is one. You shall love the LORD your God with all your heart and with all your soul and with all your might" (Deut 6:4–5). These three men were emboldened to make such a radical confession by the tales they had heard of God's mightiest deeds. They knew of how he had created the world from nothing, of the Egyptian plagues, the Angel of Death, and the Red Sea. They knew of Jericho, of the day the sun and moon paused their trail across the sky. They knew of Goliath's doom at Elah and Elijah's victory on Carmel. They knew the mighty acts of Yahweh and were convinced beyond all doubt that God could be as powerful then as he had been in centuries past (cf. Ps 119:11)!

## DANIEL 3:19–30

Their response sent Nebuchadnezzar into a violent rage once again (cf. Prov 16:14; 20:2). The text says, "the expression of his face was changed against Shadrach, Meshach, and Abednego," indicating a red-

26. P. W. Coxon, "Daniel III 17: A Linguistic and Theological Problem," *VT* 26 (1976): 408–9.

27. Most translations render 3:17 with the phrase "he [God] will rescue" (NIV), but Miller notes the Aramaic imperfect is better translated "he may rescue," (*Daniel*, 119).

28. Jerome, *Daniel*, 38.

29. "The confessors know a God who makes Nebuchadnezzar's goldplated statue look tawdry," (Goldingay, *Daniel*, 73).

faced, eyes bulging, neck veins popping, white saliva in the corners of his mouth type of rage. The order came to heat the furnace "seven times hotter," likely accomplished with additional air and fuel.[30] It would have been technically impossible to even *double* the furnace's temperature back then, let alone make it seven times hotter. The phrase is thus a hyperbole meaning something along the lines of "as hot as possible." Recall that "seven" in Scripture "is used to signify completeness or totality"[31] (cf. Prov 24:16; 26:16). With that, the king's "mighty men" (likely war veterans who had distinguished themselves in combat) bound and threw them into the furnace. They didn't even take the time to strip Shadrach, Meshach, and Abednego of their clothes (cf. Ps 22:18; Mark 15:24), meaning they would have caught fire more quickly. The scene becomes more abhorrent when Nebuchadnezzar's henchmen were killed by the furnace's severe heat as they threw them in (cf. Prov 14:17). Shadrach, Meshach, and Abednego had no chance of coming out alive. If it were possible to go below a 0.00% chance of survival, those would have been their odds.

"Then King Nebuchadnezzar was astonished" (3:24). I'd say so! "Surely, my eyes deceive me," he apparently thought. As the Babylonian despot gazed into the conflagration to witness the suffering of his rebellious administrators, he noticed they were no longer bound. Moreover, they were unharmed, walking around, and there was a fourth person with them in the furnace, one whose "appearance" was "like a son of the gods."

Who was this mysterious fourth person? An angel? The pre-incarnate Christ? It's difficult to imagine a pagan king claiming to see the NT Jesus in the flames as the KJV indicates.[32] It seems settled that he was speaking words consistent with Aramaic paganism.[33] The rabbis in the Talmud

30. Nebuchadnezzar, in his irrational rage, actually did these men a favor. Heating the furnace hotter would have shortened their suffering (Maclaren, *Expositions*, 60). Angry tyrants are seldom rational.

31. DBI 774.

32. The KJV's translation "Son of God" is grammatically indefensible (Young, *Daniel*, 94).

33. Montgomery, *Daniel*, 214–16.

said it was Gabriel the angel (b. *Pesah* 118a–b), Nebuchadnezzar actually confessed later on that (from his perspective) God had "sent his angel" (3:28; cf. Pss 34:7; 91:11; Matt 18:10; Heb 1:14), and this is consistent with how the OT speaks of angels (cf. Gen 6:2, 4; Deut 32:8; Job 1:6; 2:1; 38:7; Pss 29:1; 89:6). Even conservative scholars are hesitant to see this as a manifestation of the pre-incarnate Christ.[34] I don't blame them, and I can appreciate their desire to exercise restraint when we can't be sure.

But neither do I see anything wrong with affirming the traditional Christian interpretation, that this fourth person was the pre-incarnate Christ. It misses the point to say Nebuchadnezzar could not have meant his statement to refer to Jesus. The pagan king cannot be expected to have had perfect understanding of God's nature. He may have only meant the fourth person appeared to be "divine," but all the same spoke greater truth than he realized when he called the fourth figure one "like a son of the gods." It certainly wouldn't have been the first time such happened in Scripture (e.g. John 11:49–52; 18:37).[35]

In the end, the bigger point to be pressed is that God, in some form, was with these men in their suffering. He did not deliver them *from* the fire, but *in* the fire, a fulfillment of his promise: "When you pass through the waters, I will be with you; and through the rivers, they shall not overwhelm you; when you walk through fire you shall not be burned, and the flame shall not consume you" (Isa 43:2; cf. Ps 66:12). Jesus came to earth as Immanuel, "God with us" (Matt 1:23). It may be unclear whether the second person of the Godhead was with these men in the fiery furnace, but we know for certain that someone sent from God was there. We also know that the final thing Jesus said to his followers was "I will be with you always, even until the end of this age" (Matt 28:20 NCV; cf. Ps 23:4–5).

---

34. For example, Baldwin says the KJV's translation, one "implying a pre-incarnation appearance of Christ, is probably not correct here," (*Daniel*, 106, n. 2).

35. "Remembering that 1 Corinthians 10:1-4 expressly states that Christ was with Moses in the wilderness, we should not be surprised if it were Christ, the second person of the Trinity, who was in the midst of the fiery furnace," (Schaeffer, *No Little People*, 167).

Throughout the OT, we are told that fire represents the divine presence (Exod 3:2; 13:21; 24:17; Deut 4:11–12; Ps 18:8), and that fire cannot help but praise the Lord (Ps 148:8). So when I read Dan 3, I can't help but think of Uncle Remus' folk tale, *Brer Rabbit and the Tar Baby*. Nebuchadnezzar foolishly thought that casting these Israelites into the fire would put them beyond their God's ability to save. But the Lord of heaven, *whose very presence is inside the fire and makes even the flames to praise him,* essentially taunted the Babylonian king as the furnace was heated.

"Bred en bawn in a brier-patch, Brer Fox."

There is no place where we can escape God's presence (Ps 139:7–12), nothing can separate us from his love (Rom 8:38–39) or his deliverance (Ps 68:20), and we have no reason to fear death itself since he has promised to personally lead us across the River (Ps 48:14). While in prison, Dietrich Bonhoeffer wrote, "I trust in your grace and commit my life wholly into your hands. Do with me according to your will and as is best for me. Whether I live or die, I am with you and you, my God, are with me. Lord, I wait for your salvation and for your kingdom. Amen."[36] As countless other martyrs have discovered through the ages, God is always present in the furnace of affliction.[37]

When the three men walked out of the furnace, the power of God's miraculous deliverance was demonstrated in that their hair was not singed, their clothes were not burned, and they didn't even reek of smoke. I find that last detail to be particularly amazing. During one of my summer

36. Dietrich Bonhoeffer, *Letters and Papers from Prison*, ed. Eberhard Bethge (New York: Macmillan, 1972), 142.

37. During the Maccabean revolt, a dying Mattathias urged his sons to remember "Hananiah, Azariah, and Mishael believed and [how they] were saved from the flame" (1 Macc 2:59). This story also featured prominently in the artwork of the Roman catacombs where early Christians buried their dead, and a common prayer for the dearly departed was this: "Deliver, O Lord, the soul of your servant as you delivered the three youths from the furnace of fire," (Collins, *Daniel*, 194).

internships in college, my housing was in a basement apartment with one solitary window. The occupant before me had smoked quite heavily, and since there was virtually no ventilation, the pungent stench of cigarettes lingered in the air. I don't smoke now and didn't then, but everything I owned quickly absorbed the odor. That these three men's clothes did not reek of smoke speaks to the absolute totality of God's protection, punctuated with the statement that everyone "saw that the fire had not had any power over the bodies of those men" (3:27).

The story ends with the king praising Shadrach, Meshach, and Abednego for their courage and resolve not to dishonor their God by committing idolatry, and he gave all three a promotion. Maybe it's just me, but I get the impression Nebuchadnezzar's words were laced with more than a little fear at the notion of having offended so powerful a God. "Now it was no longer a mere picture in a dream or words in a sermon, but was here before him as a political and personal force to be reckoned with in the affairs of his own realm."[38] The king went so far as to decree that those who blasphemed this God would be dismembered and their homes "renovated" into a latrine. But Nebuchadnezzar was not yet totally and exclusively converted to the worship of Yahweh. "To him God was still the tribal deity of the three men,"[39] and the king was still forcing religious conformity on pain of death.

God and Nebuchadnezzar had a few more rounds to go.

38. Wallace, *The Lord Is King*, 69.

39. Hailey, *Daniel*, 66.

## TALKING POINTS

IT IS PATHETICALLY common for political leaders to hijack religion for their own purposes, and often via "unity" as Nebuchadnezzar did here. Babylon's famous tower had been an ill-advised attempt at unity (Gen 11:1–9), and unity was the reason Jeroboam placed his twin idols at Dan and Bethel (1 Kgs 12:25–33). Baldwin relates how President Kwame Nkrumah of Ghana erected a statue of himself outside the parliament building in Accra with this inscription: "Seek ye first the political kingdom and all other things shall be added unto you."[40] Don't be so foolish to believe that such would never happen in the U.S.[41] The values of tolerance and acceptance (biblical values to be sure, Rom 15:5–7) have become gods, and the present administration is hell-bent on commanding worship to them. Forcing companies to violate their conscience and fund abortive medicine in the name of "tolerance" and "women's health" isn't far removed from Dan 3. The first two commandments forbid idolatry; the sixth prohibits murder. What law will we obey? Which g/God will we serve? Will we kneel before the image of the beast (Rev 13:12, 15)? Any government or authority figure, totalitarian or democratic, is capable of Nebuchadnezzar's folly. The state is God's servant (Rom 13:4), but not always the church's friend, so Christians must guard against becoming too entangled with it lest our testimony and integrity become compromised, and we too are made to drink the cup of God's wrath (Rev 14:10–11). "The duty of believers is to remind the state of [its] divine limitation. They are to do it by words and, if necessary, by the laying down of their lives."[42]

---

40. Baldwin, *Daniel*, 99, n. 1. Add to this the words of Baldur von Schirach, leader of Hitler Youth in Nazi Germany, written in 1936: "Whoever serves Adolf Hitler, the Führer, serves Germany, and whoever serves Germany serves God."

41. "Despots have no monopoly of imperious intolerance. A democracy is more cruel and more impatient of singularity, and especially of religious singularity, than any despot," (Maclaren, *Expositions*, 58).

42. James Montgomery Boice, *Daniel* (Grand Rapids: Zondervan, 1989), 47.

THE FIERY FURNACE episode is not a promise that God will always rescue his people from trial. Rather, the story illustrates how there is something more important than our deliverance: the glory of God. Shadrach, Meshach, and Abednego had no intention of bowing before the statute if given a second chance, but they made it explicit that their obedience was not dependent on what God would do. Of more interest to them than their own deliverance was God magnifying himself. By allowing things to go as far as they did,[43] God indeed maximized the praise he received from the Babylonians and the thanksgiving from these three Hebrew children. So it should be with us. When trouble comes our way, we cannot possibly know how it will end, but we must resolve to honor God in all things. There is something more important than preserving our lives or minimizing our suffering, and it's making much of the One who is present with us in the flames. At the end of one of his lectures on Dan 3, Calvin prayed, "Grant us also to learn to neglect and despise our lives, especially for the testimony of thy glory; and may we be prepared to depart as soon as thou callest us from this world."[44]

AS GOD'S PEOPLE LIVING in a hostile culture, the attitude of these three men is worth our reflection. Their resistance and refusal to disobey God was silent at first; it did not gain verbal expression until they were summoned before the king. There, they were bold and defiant, but they were not insulting. They spoke plainly and resolutely. They neither engaged in verbal gymnastics, nor were they hostile.[45] This is a

43. "Instead of commanding their immediate execution, as in the case of the Magi (ch. ii. 12), Providence inclined [Nebuchadnezzar] to command the recusants to be *brought* before him, so that their noble 'testimony' for God might be given before the world powers 'against them' (Matt x. 18), to the edification of the Church in all ages," (Robert Jamieson, A. R. Fausset, and David Brown, *A Commentary Critical, Experimental and Practical on the Old and New Testament*, vol. 4 [Grand Rapids: Eerdmans, 1948], 397).

44. Calvin, *Daniel*, 1:232.

45. "For they did these things not for the sake of contention but for the love of wisdom;

reminder that, when called to take a stand for the Lord, we are not to be rude, condescending, or otherwise make more obnoxious the fragrance of Christ to those perishing (2 Cor 2:15–16). Rather, there is much to be said for following the example of Jesus himself; "When they hurled their insults at him, he did not retaliate; when he suffered, he made no threats. Instead, he entrusted himself to him who judges justly" (1 Pet 2:23 NIV). Our attitude and behavior when under trial is a powerful testimony to the glory and love of God. When called to actually speak in our own defense, we need not worry about saying "the right thing." Jesus promised to give us "a mouth of wisdom," that "not a hair" on our heads will perish until we have fulfilled all that God has planned for us to do,[46] and "by your endurance you will gain your lives" (Luke 21:12–19; cf. John 17:4). Therefore, when under attack, be ever cognizant of what you can do to bring great glory to God, instead of inflating a false sense of martyrdom and proudly playing the victim.[47]

---

not of defiance but of devotion; not being puffed up with pride but on fire with zeal. For great indeed is the blessing of a hope in God," (Chrysostom, *Homilies Concerning the Statues* 6.13).

46. "A servant of God is immortal until his work has been completed," (Ferguson, *Daniel*, 141).

47. "The courteous but determined refusal of the Hebrews should be carefully observed. They had obeyed 'the powers that be' as far as conscience permitted. They journeyed to the Plain of Dura. And right at the point where conscience shouted, 'no further!' they rejected the temptation to be arrogant in their nonconformity. As Daniel before them had been courteous in his request to follow his convictions, so these three verbally acknowledge Nebuchadnezzar as king, while committing their ultimate allegiance to the King of kings alone," (Desmond Ford, *Daniel* [Nashville: Southern Publishing, 1978], 107).

# 4

# I'M GONNA KILL MYSELF

Someone in my life, one I used to think was my friend, I recently learned is my enemy. Now I hate him. I realize "hate" is a strong word, but I hate him all the same. Of all the people I've ever known, no one else has caused me more grief or aggravation. No one else has caused me so many restless nights. No one has opposed me, maligned me, or backstabbed me like this guy. I thought he was my friend, that he was on my side—an ally. But now I know better.

When I learned of his betrayal, the rage and disappointment I felt were crippling. How had I been so blind to his treachery? How did I let this happen? How could he treat someone like this? Had he no conscience?

That person—once my friend, but now my enemy—is my ego.

Over the last year, I've come to see the ego as a powerful force that hijacks all that is good and decent within us. To say the ego is selfish isn't entirely accurate; a selfish person always does what's best for himself, but my ego is skilled at convincing me to do things that are decidedly *not* in my best interests (Prov 16:18). My ego takes credit for my every accomplishment, and also for others I had little or nothing to do with. My ego exacerbates every crisis as a conspiracy against me, though they often prove to be misunderstandings. My ego commandeers my spiritual growth by making everyone else but me responsible for my sins. I hate my ego, and I'd love nothing more than to kill it.

Which is another way of saying, "I need to kill myself."

In his famous book, *The Cost of Discipleship*, Bonhoeffer wrote the immortal words, "When Christ calls a man, he bids him come and die."[1] That quote is a restatement of Jesus' call, "If anyone would come after me, let him deny himself and take up his cross daily and follow me" (Luke 9:23; cf. Matt 16:24; Mark 8:34). Paul put it another way: "I have been crucified with Christ and I no longer live, but Christ lives in me" (Gal 2:20 NIV).

Human pride is deeply rooted in all of us since few of us are very willing to admit that it is a problem. C. S. Lewis said there is no other sin of which we are more unconscious in ourselves.[2] In his autobiography, Benjamin Franklin wrote:

> In reality, there is, perhaps, no one of our national passions so hard to subdue as *pride*. Disguise it, struggle with it, beat it down, stifle it, mortify it as much as one pleases, it is still alive ... even if I could conceive that I had completely overcome it, I should probably be proud of my humility.[3]

So far, Nebuchadnezzar had witnessed God's ability to make known the future and protect his servants from the power of fire. But he had yet to die to self and kneel submissively before God, to allow the nature of God to infect his whole life. If God cannot have the whole man, then he is uninterested in everything else about us.

This chapter confronts us with what it really means to be in a right state of mind and a right state with God. Nebuchadnezzar believed himself to be the captain of his own fate and the engine of his own prosperity. In so doing, he lost his mind and his kingdom; both were restored only when he turned "to heaven" (4:34). For us, this story is a powerful reminder of

1. Dietrich Bonhoeffer, *The Cost of Discipleship*, 2nd ed. (New York: Macmillan, 1959), 79.

2. C. S. Lewis, *Mere Christianity* (New York, Macmillan, 1943), 94.

3. Benjamin Franklin, *The Autobiography of Benjamin Franklin*, ed. Peter Conn (Philadelphia: Univ. of Pennsylvania Press, 2005), 74.

the need to kill our egos, to die to self, to take up our cross *daily*. Without doing so, we cannot be in our right mind; we cannot inherit heaven's kingdom without bowing before God's throne.

## DANIEL 4:1–9

The opening of Dan 4 reads like a personal letter "From the Desk of the King." It is a declaration Nebuchadnezzar sent "to all peoples, nations, and languages." The king expressed the letter's purpose: to declare the "signs and wonders" that God had done for him. As a whole, the letter bears many similarities to royal correspondence of the period (cf. Ezra 7:12). Given what follows, Baldwin suggests we "think of it as a confession made in a kind of open letter."[4] The lesson Nebuchadnezzar would learn in this story is the one he proclaims in 4:3: "His [God's] kingdom is an everlasting kingdom, and his dominion endures from generation to generation."

Some scholars have a hard time believing the events of this chapter. They cannot understand why Nebuchadnezzar would issue a proclamation like this, nor (so they claim) is there any evidence such a proclamation was ever issued. "As an edict the document is historically absurd; it has no similar in the history of royal conversions nor in ancient imperial edicts."[5] Furthermore, they are incredulous at the thought of a pagan king converting to the worship of the true God, and they allege that the account of Nebuchadnezzar losing his mind is a distortion of something that actually happened to a latter king of Babylon, Nabonidus.

We'll discuss this last allegation later, but scholars argue that there is no historical corroboration of this proclamation or of a seven-year absence during Nebuchadnezzar's reign.[6] However, we know virtually nothing about the final thirty years of Nebuchadnezzar's reign. The Babylonian

---

4. Baldwin, *Daniel*, 107.

5. Montgomery, *Daniel*, 222. "But observe how many events recorded in the Scriptures have no parallels in secular history and are yet accepted by us," (Leupold, *Daniel*, 168).

6. Collins, *Daniel*, 228.

Chronicle ends with his 11th year (594 B.C.) and doesn't resume until Nabonidus' day. All we have from this part of Nebuchadnezzar's life is the biblical record, so this story would obviously sound fishy to anyone already prejudiced against God's Word.

This story likely takes place near the end of Nebuchadnezzar's life since the bulk of his building program had been completed (4:30).[7] He had retired from the field of battle, and he was enjoying the peaceful years of his reign now that his empire dominated the known world. None rivaled Babylon's power at this time. No wonder, then, that he was "at ease" and "prospering" (4:4). This latter word can be translated "flourishing" (HCSB); it literally means "in full leaf"[8] and is "a rather appropriate word in light of the dream the king was about to describe."[9]

But it was during this season of life that he had another dream, and he was again "alarmed" (4:5; cf. 5:6, 9–10; 7:15, 28). He called for his wise men and told them the dream (unlike the first time), but they were again useless to explain it. "At last Daniel came in" (4:8). Why had Daniel not been summoned at the beginning? Was Nebuchadnezzar still trusting in his fraudulent dreamologists and false gods? Possibly, but the answer may be as simple as Daniel was actually summoned along with the other wise men, but he was the last to arrive for whatever reason.[10] After all, the king quickly acknowledged him as "chief of the magicians" (cf. 2:49) and that no mystery was "too difficult" for him (4:9). Regardless of why, I'm inclined to see Daniel's delayed arrival as providential; it gave the king another opportunity to witness the ineptness of his wise men.

---

7. Wood (*Daniel*, 99) places the king's dream between his 30th and 35th year (i.e. 575–569). As in Dan 3, the LXX claims this event occurred in the king's 18th year (587–586), the same year that Jerusalem was totally destroyed, but this is likely an unjustified addition to the text. Other suggestions include 583, making the seven years coincide with the hiatus in the siege of Tyre (Archer, "Daniel," 59–60).

8. HALOT 5:1983.

9. Edward P. Myers, Neale T. Pryor, and David R. Rechtin, *Daniel* (Searcy, AR: Resource Publications, 2012), 138).

10. Coffman, *Daniel*, 66. Wood believes a divine revelation restrained Daniel (*Daniel*, 105).

## DANIEL 4:10–18

In the dream (cf. Job 33:15–18), the king saw a towering tree, "visible to the end of the whole earth" (4:11). The tree provided food and shelter (cf. Pss 1:3; 104:16–17; Jer 17:8); Lucas believes the imagery of Eden's Tree of Life may lie behind the tree in this dream.[11] Nebuchadnezzar is later identified with the tree, meaning the king saw himself as the "keeper of the cosmos,"[12] a title only God can rightfully claim (Col 1:17). After the tree is described, "a watcher, a holy one" (i.e. an angel) descended from heaven and called for the tree to be chopped down, its branches hewn, and its leaves and fruit scattered. Its stump and roots, however, were to remain; the stump would be preserved with a band of iron and bronze. Meanwhile, Nebuchadnezzar would experience heaven's dew, eat grass like an ox, and lose his mind[13] for a period of "seven times" (NIV).

This decree from the watcher was given so "that the living may know that the Most High rules the kingdom of men and gives it to whom he will and sets over it the lowliest of men" (4:17; cf. 1 Sam 2:8; Ps 113:7–8; Luke 1:52). This is the clear teaching of Scripture, that God raises up rulers—large and small—and gives them power as a stewardship (Rom 13:1). Though rulers have free will, God nonetheless can manipulate them according to his purposes (Prov 19:21; 21:1). Simply put, it is God's prerogative to establish people in positions of authority at any time for any reason. Schemes, plots, coups, and elections make it seem as if we are responsible for our own leaders, but the Bible maintains a different reality.

## DANIEL 4:19–27

Daniel seemed to know immediately the significance of the king's dream. As it had the king, the dream "alarmed him" (4:19), but he was

11. Lucas, *Daniel*, 110.

12. Longman, *Daniel*, 119.

13. The word translated "be changed" (4:16) was sometimes used in Akkadian literature for mental derangement (Hill, "Daniel," 94.).

also "dismayed," i.e. embarrassed or perplexed.[14] Daniel's alarm rendered him speechless for a brief while.[15] Nebuchadnezzar encouraged him not to hesitate in sharing it (cf. 1 Sam 3:17); Daniel's affection for the king is evident in his wish that the dream apply to Nebuchadnezzar's enemies (cf. 2 Sam 18:32), but Daniel knew better.[16] As Daniel explained, the tree represented Nebuchadnezzar—kings and nations were often depicted as mighty trees in OT poetry (cf. Ps 37:35; Isa 2:13; 10:34; Jer 22:15; Ezek 17:22–24; 31:3; Hos 14:5–7; Amos 2:9; Zech 11:1–2). Herodotus says Xerxes had a dream of his being crowned with olive leaves, and "the shoots spread over the whole earth," which the Magi interpreted as an omen that Xerxes would conquer the world (*Histories* 7.19).

Daniel affirmed that Nebuchadnezzar had become strong and great, but the "decree of the Most High" via the watcher was that he would be driven from civilization and into the wild. This would be for a period of "seven times" (NIV) until the king confessed "that the Most High rules the kingdom of men and gives it to whom he will" (4:25). While he was away, his kingdom would be preserved for him as symbolized by the band around the stump[17] (cf. Isa 6:13; 11:1).

At the end of the dream's explanation, Daniel begged Nebuchadnezzar to act preemptively so that the dream did not come to pass, and that he "might continue to be successful" (4:27 NCV). Specifically,

14. Young, *Daniel*, 106.

15. The KJV's "one hour" is misleading; the Aramaic simply means a "short time" (HALOT 5:2000).

16. "A less courageous man than Daniel would have blunted the edge with which God was trying to pierce the heart in order to begin the healing process," (Wallace, *The Lord Is King*, 82). "Whilst pitying the king, he uncompromisingly pronounces his sentence of punishment. Let ministers steer the mean between, on the one hand, fulminations against sinners under the pretext of zeal, without any symptom of compassion; and, on the other, flattery of sinners under the pretext of moderation," (Jamieson, *Commentary*, 4:403).

17. Baldwin, *Daniel*, 113; cf. Myers, *Daniel*, 141. Longman acknowledges, however, that interpreting the band on the stump as preservation of the kingdom is somewhat weak and "would be strengthened if such a practice were known from the ancient Near East, but no such evidence is available," (*Daniel*, 119).

Nebuchadnezzar was exhorted to "break off" his sin by "practicing righteousness" (cf. Acts 26:20), i.e. "showing mercy to the oppressed." "If a king judges poor people fairly, his government will continue forever" (Prov 29:14).[18] Evidently, the king had not exhibited such kindness and justice to the disenfranchised of his empire. As remains the case today, a healthy relationship with God is defined in part by our concern for "the least of these" (Matt 25:31–46; cf. Mic 6:8; Jas 1:27).

## DANIEL 4:28–33

We aren't told Nebuchadnezzar's immediate response. Rather, the narrative skips ahead a year to when the king was on his palace roof (an ominous note for those familiar with 2 Sam 11:2), gazing at the splendor of the city and empire he had built. Nebuchadnezzar is remembered by historians, not only for his success as a military leader, but also for his accomplishments as a builder—in fact, the POWs he brought back likely provided the slave labor necessary to power his massive building projects. Babylon had declined over the many centuries until Nabopolassar, and then Nebuchadnezzar, restored it. Many of the bricks used in Nebuchadnezzar's building programs were stamped with his name.

Nebuchadnezzar constructed canals so that the Euphrates flowed through the city, docks to service ships and passengers, and a 400-foot-long bridge across the Euphrates, connecting the east and west portions of Babylon.[19] His palace was luxuriously decorated with bronze thresholds and massive beams made of Lebanon cedars.[20] The king commissioned

---

18. "Unfortunately the sinful pride of the human race has blinded mankind to the true function of political institutions—that they should be self-consciously the instruments of God's just rule on the earth. Despite this, their rule is sanctioned by the Lord even if not approved by Him in its particular manifestations," (Eugene H. Merrill, "A Theology of Ezekiel and Daniel" in *A Biblical Theology of the Old Testament*, ed. Roy B. Zuck [Chicago: Moody, 1991], 391).

19. Robert Koldewey, *The Excavations of Babylon*, trans. Agnes S. Johns (London: Macmillan, 1914), 197.

20. Wiseman, *Nebuchadrezzar and Babylon*, 51–73.

the Hanging Gardens of Babylon as a gift for his wife (that was the *last* time he forgot their anniversary!). With its lush plants, waterfalls, and orchards, the Hanging Gardens were the first of Babylon's two entries to the Seven Wonders of the Ancient World. Its city walls were the second. The outer wall alone was nearly seventeen miles long, forty feet high, 25 feet thick, and "wide enough at the top for chariots to pass."[21]

It's been said, "It's not bragging if it's true," but such a statement splatters against the windshield of this passage like a bug. Nebuchadnezzar's words were true, yet they were also boastful and arrogant before the Most High. No sooner had he spoken than heaven rang out:

> This is the verdict on you, King Nebuchadnezzar: Your kingdom is taken from you. You will be driven out of human company and live with the wild animals. You will eat grass like an ox. The sentence is for seven seasons, enough time to learn that the High God rules human kingdoms and puts whomever he wishes in charge.
>
> Dan 4:31-32 Msg

That's exactly what happened. Nebuchadnezzar was driven away from civilization, ate and lived like a cow,[22] his body drenched with dew, and his hair and nails grew to resemble a bird's feathers and claws. Being exposed to the elements would have been horrible—temperatures in that area of the world can soar into the triple digits during the summer and drop below freezing in the winter.[23] His condition is often said to have been a form of lycanthropy, a mental disorder in which the sufferer believes and acts as if he is an animal. Lycanthropy has afflicted such notables

---

21. Miller, *Daniel*, 140.

22. My dad was fond of quipping that Nebuchadnezzar was the first drug addict in the Bible—he was on "grass" for seven years!

23. Archer, "Daniel," 66.

as England's King George III and Bavaria's King Otto.[24] R. K. Harrison personally witnessed a case of lycanthropy in Britain 1946. The man was in his 20s and spent his time outdoors in the winter with no coat of any kind. "The only physical abnormality noted consisted of a lengthening of the hair and a coarse, thickened condition of the finger-nails. Without institutional care the patient would have manifested precisely the same physical conditions as those mentioned in Daniel 4:33."[25]

I have no reservation in believing the plausibility of this theory, but the biblical text plainly says what happened—whether natural or miraculous—was from the hand of God. Put another way, the text is interested only in the divine cause of Nebuchadnezzar's madness.

As noted earlier, virtually nothing is known about the last thirty years of Nebuchadnezzar's reign, so this story cannot be easily corroborated with historical records. But there is a certain cuneiform text, one very fragmented, that mentions Nebuchadnezzar suffering from a mental disorder in his final years, one that possibly forced him to leave Babylon, leaving his son, Amel-Marduk, to reign in his absence.[26] Again, the text is so fragmented that it's hard to know for sure its relation to Dan 4. Jewish tradition, however, corroborates that Amel-Marduk reigned while his father was insane; once Nebuchadnezzar returned, he threw his son in prison. When the king actually died and Amel-Marduk assumed the throne, he mutilated his father's corpse and had it drug through Babylon's streets.[27] If only his father had taken him fishing more...

However, this may not be the only historical record of these events. Among the discovery of the Dead Sea Scrolls was a text in Aramaic now known as the "Prayer of Nabonidus." It reads:

---

24. Lucas, *Daniel*, 111.

25. R. K. Harrison, *Introduction to the Old Testament* (Grand Rapids: Eerdmans, 1969), 1116.

26. Wiseman, *Nebuchadrezzar and Babylon*, 102–3.

27. Ginzberg, *Legends of the Jews*, 4:339.

> Words of the prayer which Nabonidus, king of the la[nd of Babylon, [the great] king, prayed [when he was afflicted] by a malignant inflammation, by decree of the G[od Most] High, in Teiman. [I, Nabonidus,] was afflicted [by a malignant inflammation] for seven years, and was banished far [from men, until I prayed to the God Most High] and an exorcist forgave my sin. He was a Je[w] from [the exiles, who said to me:] Make a proclamation in writing, so that glory, exal[tation and honour] be given to the name of the G[od Most High. And I wrote as follows: When] [I was afflicted by a malig[nant] inflammation, [and remained] in Teiman, [by decree of the God Most High, I] prayed for seven years [to all] the gods of silver and gold, [of bronze and iron,] of wood, or stone and of clay, because [I thought] that they were gods [ ... ][28]

There are several differences between this story and the one in Dan 4—the disease is different, the Jewish "exorcist" or prophet is unnamed—but there are also striking similarities as you can see. So much so that some have claimed this story is the original, and the biblical text is an inaccurate reflection of it.[29] However, this is no more likely than the opposite: this story concerning Nabonidus is a corrupted, inaccurate reflection—a faulty memory—of what really happened to Nebuchadnezzar in Dan 4.[30] Baldwin points out that no one has proven Daniel's version to be *in*correct,[31]

---

28. Florentino García Martínez, *The Dead Sea Scrolls Translated*, 2nd ed., trans. Wilfred G. E. Watson (Grand Rapids: Eerdmans, 1996), 289.

29. "There is general consensus that 4QPrNab [i.e. "Prayer of Nabonidus"] establishes the view that Daniel 4 is ultimately based on traditions about Nabonidus," (Collins, *Daniel*, 218). Contra Henze: "The discrepancies between the Prayer of Nabonidus and the tale of Nebuchadnezzar's madness are significant enough to exclude the possibility of a direct literary relationship," (Matthias Henze, *The Madness of King Nebuchadnezzar* [Leiden: Brill, 1999], 68). Lucas urges "caution" in drawing conclusions (*Daniel*, 107), and justifiably so.

30. Andrew Steinmann, "The Chicken and the Egg: A New Proposal for the Relationship Between the Prayer of Nabonidus and the Book of Daniel," *RevQ* 20 (2002): 557–70.

31. Baldwin, *Daniel*, 118.

and since this chapter affirms God's sovereignty and power over all men, I will assume the burden of proof doesn't fall on the Most High.

## DANIEL 4:34–37

Throughout the chapter, there is repeated mention of "seven times" as the duration of Nebuchadnezzar's punishment. Beginning with the LXX and Josephus (*Antiquities* 10.217), most every interpreter has understood this to mean seven years (cf. Rev 12:6, 14). But I agree with Hailey, who sees "seven times" as symbolic of perfection and completion, "an indefinite time for the complete accomplishment of a divine purpose." He argues that this was an indefinite period lasting until Nebuchadnezzar finally acknowledged God's sovereignty. [32]This is corroborated by 4:17, 25, 32 and by the phrase, "At the end of the days" (4:34).

There is something to be said for Nebuchadnezzar's sudden return to reason when he turned his gaze to heaven (Ps 123:1; Isa 45:22). We are never less in our right mind than when our ego controls our whole person. It was ego that drove a young man to brazenly request his inheritance while his father was still living. So starved that he was eating pig slop, "he came to himself" (Luke 15:17) and realized his father's slaves lived like kings compared to his present circumstances. Reflecting on Dan 4, Fewell notes, "A man who thinks he is like a god must become a beast to learn that he is only a human being."[33] I would add that a man, whether a prince or a pauper, is happiest when he bows in submission before the Father.

Nebuchadnezzar had his empire and power restored to him, but only after he had knelt in submission before the throne.[34] In his doxology,

---

32. Hailey, *Daniel*, 77, 81; cf. Young, *Daniel*, 105.

33. Danna Nolan Fewell, *Circle of Sovereignty*, 2nd ed. (Nashville: Abingdon, 1991), 72.

34. "The antidote to Nebuchadnezzar's pride was not merely a new knowledge in the head, but a new exultation in the heart. His praise and exultation reveal the wakening of faith, and the gladness that God ruled the future with the omnipotent grace to establish his plan and humble the proud. He was satisfied with God's prerogative to do as he pleases in the sovereign freedom of his justice and grace," (John Piper, *Future Grace*, rev. ed. [Colorado Springs: Multnomah, 2012], 89).

he acknowledged God's everlasting dominion and eternal kingdom (cf. Pss 115:3; 145:13). "All the inhabitants of the earth are accounted as nothing" (cf. Isa 40:17) does not mean God is unconcerned with us (John 3:16), but that no one can come close to rivaling his power and glory. The greatest of men have as much chance of dethroning God as an ant has against my boot. "None can stay his hand" (4:35; cf. Ps 33:10–11; Isa 14:27; 43:13) means no one has the right to question God's justice when he judges the proud and the wicked, "for all his works are right and his ways are just" (4:37; cf. Ps 111:7). The phrase is "derived from the custom of striking children on the hand in chastising them."[35]

Hailey notes that one thing is lacking in Nebuchadnezzar's decree: the confession that Daniel's God is the only God. For those reasons, he seems unsure whether the king died in a right relationship with God. But he holds out hope since: 1.) the final thirty years of the king's reign aren't recorded, and 2.) Daniel's faithful influence "might have led him to a complete acceptance of Jehovah as the only true God, and to a complete rejection of all false gods."[36] Obviously, the final word on Nebuchadnezzar's soul is not ours to give, so we await the final judgment to know the rest of the story.

NEBUCHADNEZZAR HAD a rather healthy ego. So do I, and you also. Our ego loves to promote us, but it is not our friend. The prince of this world has infiltrated our ego, and through it he seeks to corrupt and destroy all that is good in life (John 10:10). It's not enough to modify our behavior to appear more humble; we must ruthlessly and regularly put the ego to death. Maybe our tree needs to fall so that we can abandon ourselves to another tree, a cross that births glory out of shame. "When Christ calls a man, he bids him come and die," for Christ cannot bring us

35. C. F. Keil, *Biblical Commentary on the Book of Daniel*, trans. M. G. Easton (Grand Rapids: Eerdmans, 1949), 160–61.

36. Hailey, *Daniel*, 86–89.

life as long as our ego is alive and working for our destruction. But the very moment we die to self and take up the King's tree, we become heirs of a kingdom far greater than any on earth.

There is a message of hope in the fact that Nebuchadnezzar, though forced to live in the wild, and vulnerable to all that could happen in such circumstances, still fell under the protection of heaven. God had promised to preserve his throne, and he did so. On how many occasions has God preserved our lives so that we might finally turn our hearts to him to trust and obey? "Or do you show contempt for the riches of his kindness, forbearance and patience, not realizing that God's kindness is intended to lead you to repentance?" (Rom 2:4 NIV). Live not another moment without dying to self and discovering the grace of life as a servant of King Jesus!

## TALKING POINTS

AMONG THE MOST fundamental declarations of the book of Daniel is that earthly governments are but tools in the hand of the Lord. As Paul put it, governments "have been instituted by God" (Rom 13:1), but this does not mean every government carries God's stamp of approval. Every political leader must learn this and rehearse it often. The medieval notion of the "divine right of kings" has given way to a more modern attitude that government can't do wrong; President Nixon is a striking example of this. Government will always be corrupt to some degree because of sin's plague on the human race. But those Christians who hold political office have a special responsibility to hold to a biblical paradigm of civic power—namely, that government ideally exists to be God's instrument for good (Rom 13:4). In Dan 4, Nebuchadnezzar had forgotten his divinely-appointed responsibility to use his power for the benefit of the down-and-out and disenfranchised (4:27). Anyone who uses their power to exalt themselves rather than doing good for others (and thereby exalting God[37]) can expect to be on the receiving end of the most severe derision of heaven.

IN NOVEMBER 2000, *USA Today* reported the results of the 2000 Phoenix Wealth Management Survey of senior corporate executives with a net worth of $1 million or more. To what did they credit their prosperity? "Hard work" was cited by 99%, "intelligence and good sense" by 97%, having a "higher-than-average IQ" by 83%, "being the best in every situation" by 62%, and good ole fashioned "luck" by 32%.[38] As one can imagine, "God" or some variation wasn't mentioned at all. We've come a long way from the first Thanksgiving Declaration issued on Oct 3, 1789 by President Washington: "It is the duty of all Nations to acknowledge

37. "Earthly authorities are in the hand of God, not merely for their judgment, but for his glory," (Goldingay, *Daniel*, 97).

38. "Snapshots," *USA Today*, Nov 13, 2000.

the providence of Almighty God, to obey his will, to be grateful for his benefits, and humbly to implore his protection and favor." To whom do we attribute life's success? Nebuchadnezzar was judged severely because he took credit for what he had done, but he forgot that the breath in his lungs, the strength in his hand, and the wisdom in his mind were all gifts from above (Jas 1:17). We would do well to learn from his mistake and follow Washington's order, as well as Paul's: "Be thankful in all circumstances, for this is God's will for you who belong to Christ Jesus" (1 Thess 5:18 NLT).

I REALLY ENJOY HIKING, and if I ever lived near the mountains, I'd be hitting the trails every weekend if possible. One of the truly incredible experiences while hiking in the mountains is to behold the towering peaks at the trailhead, and then—hours later—to see how small everything is as you look down on the route you've traversed. Lakes and stands of trees that were once large, now appear so tiny. What changed? The perspective. We build egotistical kingdoms and revel in our self-importance, but if we ascend to a higher plane, the view from above exposes just how small we are. "If there is anything that we ought to get straight, it is how little we are,"[39] for "sanity begins with a realistic self-appraisal."[40] Nebuchadnezzar discovered this when he lifted his eyes to heaven, hinting "that we come to be truly in our right mind when we begin to view and value everything else in the light of heavenly realities."[41] This is why Paul encouraged us to "think about the things of heaven, not the things of earth" (Col 3:2 NLT). With our attention and affections in heaven, our passion for the kingdom of self will be undermined and eventually destroyed. Our attraction to the world's values—abusive power, selfish pleasure, or divisive unity—will wane. The things that seemed so great and intimidating to us will now appear pathetic and small. Our ability to trust God will grow stronger.

39. A. W. Tozer, *Success and the Christian* (Camp Hill, PA: WingSpread, 1994), 45.

40. Baldwin, *Daniel*, 116.

41. Wallace, *The Lord Is King*, 84.

The view "from above" puts us in our right mind.

THROUGHOUT DANIEL'S experiences with Nebuchadnezzar, the king frequently appeared volatile and paranoid, while the prophet was always cool, calm, and collected. One was a slave to his ego, the other to the Everlasting God. Your mileage may vary, but my ego loves to manufacture fear more than anything else. The more important I consider myself to be, the more I believe others are out to get me, to tear me down, to bring about my ruin and destruction. I become more paranoid and anxious the more I focus on myself rather than others (extremists and conspiracy theorists prey on fear). I foolishly buy into the notion that I can control the future, and when the future goes in a direction I didn't foresee, I become even more worried and afraid. Fear is among Satan's most effective weapons, and he cultivates it by any means necessary. Fear springs from pride (cf. Isa 51:12–13). Fear is not from God (2 Tim 1:7), but his perfect love can cast it out (1 John 4:18). The antidote to fear is faith. Turning our gaze upward to heaven, rather than inward to ourselves, mortifies our fear. Submitting to God means we trust him, and he thereby invites us to make him responsible for our every concern (1 Pet 5:6–7). When persecution comes our way, we shouldn't panic or scream about our "rights." Rather, our faith will remind us that God loves us, that he is just, that he is also sovereign, and that remarkable blessings are for those who kiss his Son and seek refuge in him (Ps 2:12). Put another way, our faith will keep us in our right mind.

# 5

# THE HANGOVER

Between the end of Dan 4 and the beginning of Dan 5, the narrator zooms ahead more than twenty years. Nebuchadnezzar died in 562 B.C., and Babylon fell to Cyrus in 539. A lot transpired in those two decades; Nebuchadnezzar's son, Amel-Marduk, ascended the throne and reigned for about two years. But he was assassinated in Aug 560 by Neriglissar, whose brief reign of four years was very tumultuous. He was succeeded by his son, Labashi-Marduk, who held on to the throne for a remarkable nine months before being assassinated in a coup. This is how Nabonidus became king in 556. As you can see, things unraveled for Babylon after Nebuchadnezzar's death.

Though separated by time, there are several points of comparison between these two chapters. Both concern very proud and arrogant kings of Babylon who dared to array themselves against the majesty of the Most High God. Both stories have the king summoning his wise men to interpret something he did not understand, and both stories demonstrate that only Daniel (by God's grace) was able to interpret. Both stories also contain notice of God's judgment on these kings. But the stories also differ since Nebuchadnezzar, though judged by God, came to his senses at the end. Belshazzar never repented of his blasphemous arrogance.

As we will later see, historical records confirm this chapter's account of Babylon's fall. God's judgment was swift and sure. Just as Isaiah had predicted many years before, Cyrus and his army overwhelmed the Babylonian Empire, and it passed into the pages of history with barely a whimper. Secular historians might claim that such happened because the Medo-Persian army under Cyrus' leadership was the superior force. But the Bible would have us confess that Babylon fell because she had been weighed in the scales of God's justice and had proven lacking. As had been the case with Sodom, sin had reached its full measure (cf. Gen 15:16; 18:20). God had had enough.

And yet, even though this story is set in the midst of a deplorable, drunken orgy, it seems Belshazzar's (and by extension, Babylon's) greatest sin was not so much his immorality as his blaspheming God and not honoring him for who he is: the Creator and Sustainer of life. There is a powerful lesson to be learned from this story. Judgment awaits all those—political dictators in Africa, Fortune 500 executives in New York, tenured professors in Oxford, and housewives in Atlanta—who lift themselves up "against the Lord of heaven" (5:23). Each one of us, if only rulers of the kingdom of self, are at grave risk of committing Belshazzar's blasphemy.

## BELSHAZZAR

For many years, it was commonly assumed Belshazzar was not a real person since no mention was ever made of him in Babylonian records. As far as history was concerned, Nabonidus was Babylon's king when it fell to Cyrus. This great silence on Belshazzar's existence prompted Ferdinand Hitzig to brazenly conclude in 1850 that he was a fictional character invented by the author of Daniel.[1]

But in 1854, a British explorer uncovered what proved to be the temple of the ancient city of Ur. Among the ruins were cylinders commemorating the temple's restoration during the reign of Nabonidus (556–539 B.C.). The cylinders contained a prayer "for the long life and good health of Nabonidus—and for his eldest son. The name of that son,

1. Ferdinand Hitzig, *Das Buch Daniel* (Leipzig: Weidman, 1850), 75.

clearly written, was Belshazzar!"[2] Since that time, some 37 texts have been accumulated, corroborating the existence of Belshazzar.

What happened is this. By about 550, Nabonidus had become pretty unpopular with many Babylonian priests. Whereas Nebuchadnezzar had been the bee's knees for his staunch support of the Marduk cult, Nabonidus promoted the cult of the moon goddess, Sin, since his mother was a priestess. This made him *persona non grata* in the capital. To keep the peace, Nabonidus took a long vacation to Tema, a rich desert oasis situated on a caravan route running from the Gulf of Aqaba to the Persian Gulf. Nabonidus went there to indulge his unpopular religious beliefs; meanwhile, *The Verse Account of Nabonidus* claims he "entrusted the kingship to ... his oldest (son), the first-born."[3] This son was Belshazzar.

Belshazzar had a pure mean-streak in him and may have been the one who assassinated his father's predecessor.[4] The Greek historian Xenophon records how Gobryas, a governor under Nabonidus, defected to the Persians when Belshazzar speared Gobryas' son in a jealous rage during a hunt; the son had bagged a bear and a lion, while Belshazzar had come up with nothing (*Cyropaedia* 4.6.1–10).

While his father was away, Belshazzar did not enjoy every regal privilege and prerogative. For example, Nabonidus retained the title of "king," while his son was known as "son of the king." Belshazzar could not replace political appointees, nor preside over the New Year's Festival, and his orders did not carry the full weight of his father's. Furthermore, Nabonidus was the one recognized as king in building inscriptions from his reign.

However, Belshazzar did receive tribute and meat sacrificed to idols (the king's prerogative in ancient times); oaths were sworn in both his

2. Alan Millard, "Daniel and Belshazzar in History," *BAR* 11/3 (1985): 75.

3. James B. Pritchard, ed., *Ancient Near Eastern Texts Relating to the Old Testament*, 3rd ed. (Princeton, NJ: Princeton Univ. Press, 1969), 313.

4. Paul-Alain Beaulieu, *The Reign of Nabonidus King of Babylon 556-539* B.C. (New Haven, CT: Yale Univ. Press, 1989), 90–92, 97, 184.

name and Nabonidus', and Belshazzar enjoyed command of half the military. "The scope of each administrative decision made by Belshazzar cannot be fully evaluated, but there is enough evidence to conclude that he was the highest administrative authority in Babylonia during Nabonidus' absence, and that in most cases he was acting with full regnal power."[5]

So why does the biblical text consider Belshazzar to be "king" in Dan 5? For all intents and purposes, he was! He was "the only ruler with whom the people dealt directly for so many years."[6] Nabonidus was an absentee king, but the royal record-keepers continued to regard him as the actual king, and his son as the crown prince. A modern-day analogy might explain things. A provision of the U.S. Constitution's 25th amendment is that the president can temporarily transfer his power to the vice president in certain circumstances (e.g. while under anesthesia). When this happens, the vice president is not officially considered to have been president of the U.S., though he technically held the power of the office for a time, if only for an hour. In every practical way, Belshazzar was king at the fall of Babylon, but his father was also the king.

For those who remain unconvinced, we may be imposing too narrow a definition on "king." In 1979, a Syrian farmer discovered a statue containing an inscription in two languages, Assyrian and Aramaic. Dating to c. 850 B.C., the Assyrian inscription alluded to the "governor of Gozan," but the Aramaic version called him "king" (Aramaic *melek*), the same word used in Dan 5 for Belshazzar. It suggests that the word encompassed more than a technical king.[7]

Another question arising from the text, one that strikes at the story's historicity, is how Belshazzar could claim Nebuchadnezzar as his "father" (5:2, 11, 13, 18; cf. "his son," 5:22). No Greek historian ever linked Nabonidus and Nebuchadnezzar as blood-kin. Nabonidus said his father

5. Ibid., 186–97.

6. Michael J. Gruenthaner, "The Last King of Babylon," *CBQ* 11 (1949): 419.

7. Millard, "Daniel and Belshazzar," 77.

was Nabubalatsuiqbi (say that three times fast and I'll give you a $2 bill). Thus, several proposals have been offered.

Wiseman suggested Nabonidus married Nebuchadnezzar's daughter, making Belshazzar Nebuchadnezzar's grandson[8] (cf. Jer 27:7). This is very plausible since "father" and "son" in Aramaic can be used of more distant ancestors/descendants (e.g. Ezra 4:15; 5:12; Dan 2:23).[9] Plus, Nebuchadnezzar married off one daughter to a general named Nergalsharusur, so it's not difficult to believe he did the same for a faithful diplomat such as Nabonidus.[10] The only issue with Wiseman's theory is that there is no hard evidence to validate it.

Another theory is derived from the Black Obelisk of Shalmaneser III, king of Assyria (859–824 B.C.). On it is a reference to Jehu, king of Israel, who is called the "son of Omri." From the biblical record, we know Omri and Jehu were no relation; Jehu, in fact, extinguished Omri's dynasty (2 Kgs 9–10). But Jehu was his indirect successor, and this may be what is meant when Nebuchadnezzar is considered Belshazzar's father, even though four kings reigned between them, and they may not have been related at all.

Before moving on, I want you to stop and realize that this is yet another example of critics incorrectly slandering the historicity of Scripture. For so many years, Dan 5 was derided since there was nary a mention in historical records of Belshazzar, but these detractors were proven wrong. "The Christian need not fear that history will ever disprove what we have recorded in our Bibles."[11] In the 19th century, Alexander Maclaren asked a rhetorical question that bears repeating: "Why should

8. Wiseman, *Nebuchadrezzar and Babylon*, 11. Leupold suggests the unlikely idea that Nabonidus married the widow of Nebuchadnezzar and adopted her child (*Daniel*, 211).

9. W. Robertson Smith lists seven ways "father" and twelve ways "son" could be understood in antiquity (*Kinship and Marriage in Early Arabia* [Cambridge: Cambridge Univ. Press, 1885], 44–46, 110–14).

10. Belshazzar may have claimed Nebuchadnezzar as his "father" because Nabonidus was so unpopular with the people (Jim McGuiggan, *The Book of Daniel* [Lubbock, TX: Sunset Institute Press, 2011], 100).

11. Ironside, *Daniel*, 80.

it not be possible for Scripture to preserve a name that secular history has not yet been ascertained to record, and why must it always be assumed that, if Scripture and cuneiform or other documents differ, it is Scripture that must go to the wall?"[12] In other words, why must Scripture—the reliability of which has been vindicated time and again—always bear the burden of proof, and not fallible, secular historians?[13]

## DANIEL 5:1–12

On the eve of Babylon's collapse, Belshazzar held a feast (cf. Isa 21:5; Jer 51:39) for a large number of the aristocracy—"thousand" here is not exact, but simply means "a lot."[14] Reading the narrative alone gives the impression that nothing was imminent, just a spoiled king having a party (cf. Esth 1:1–8). But the city of Babylon knew it was about to be attacked (though not necessarily overrun) by Cyrus' army. This feast took place on the night of Oct 12, 539. Days earlier, the Babylonian army had fallen to Cyrus at Opis, the city of Sippar had then surrendered without a fight, and Nabonidus had fled (he was later captured). Cyrus was now on his way to Babylon. Belshazzar had gathered the "Who's Who" of the city to invoke the protection of the gods so that mighty Babylon might not fall (cf. 1 Thess 5:3).[15]

Part of the revelry included something Nebuchadnezzar had never done—the sacred vessels from the Jerusalem Temple were brought in so

---

12. Maclaren, *Expositions*, 63.

13. "If you want to look very wise in the world's eyes and are willing to risk looking foolish years from now, you can make a reputation for yourself by pointing out the 'errors' in the Bible," (Boice, *Daniel*, 65).

14. DBI 865–66. The palace throne room was approximately 170 feet by 56 feet, so a thousand guests might have been quite crowded in such a space (Goldingay, *Daniel*, 108–9; cf. Koldewey, *Excavations of Babylon*, 103).

15. Baldwin believes, as is plausible, that "Belshazzar's banquet was sheer bravado, the last fling of a terrified ruler unsuccessfully attempting to drown his fears," (*Daniel*, 120). Lucas adds, "The lavishness of the feast, especially in the face of an enemy army … is probably meant to underline the king's careless hubris," (*Daniel*, 128).

that the party guests could drink from them. "The king must have lost his sense of decency to commit what is to the Oriental view a sacrilege even with the holy things of another religion."[16] These vessels would have included the 5,400 gold and silver items mentioned in Ezra 1:9–11, and had originally been commissioned by Solomon to be crafted by Hiram of Tyre (1 Kgs 7:40–50). Brought from Jerusalem and placed in the temple of Marduk, they represented the Babylonians' belief that Marduk had been victorious over Yahweh when Jerusalem had fallen (cf. 1 Sam 5:2). By drinking from these vessels, perhaps Belshazzar and his nobles were reminding Marduk of past victories and soliciting his protection now that Cyrus was at their back door.

But the fact remains that the king took what was holy and gave it to the dogs (cf. Isa 52:11). "His very act is like spitting in the eye of God."[17] While Belshazzar foolishly believed the vessels were proof of Yahweh's impotence, the exact opposite was true (cf. Ps 10:6). "The captured sacred objects of the God of Israel, were in fact the sure signs of God's victory. Israel had gone into captivity not because of the weakness of its God but because of his strength."[18]

The statement in 5:4 is notable if only because of what happened next. In their revelry, the partygoers "praised the gods of gold and silver, bronze, iron, wood, and stone." The narrator could have just as well have said "they praised the gods," but by elaborating on their composition, he highlighted how these gods were no more than impotent frauds, helpless to deliver Babylon from her doom (cf. Isa 46:5–7).

As the king and his friends exchanged toasts to the gods, a mysterious

---

16. Montgomery, Daniel, 251. "Whilst under the effects of wine, men will do what they dare not do when sober," (Jamieson, *Commentary*, 4:407); cf. Prov 20:1; 31:4.

17. Longman, *Daniel*, 137.

18. Anderson, *Signs and Wonders*, 60. Jerome relates a Jewish tradition that claims Belshazzar (mis)calculated the seventy years of the exile, and thinking they had come and gone, decided to hold this banquet to scorn the failure of Israel's God to end the exile. "Punishment, however, immediately ensued," (*Daniel*, 56; cf. b. *Megilla* 11b–12a).

hand began to write words "on the plaster of the wall of the king's palace, opposite the lampstand" (5:5). Such detail in this statement is remarkable, meaning whoever recorded this story had first-hand familiarity with the palace throne room in Babylon. When this site was excavated in 1899, it was confirmed that the walls had been covered in white gypsum.[19] There would have been several lampstands in the palace, but this one[20] is noted to convey that the writing was clearly illuminated and not in the shadows. The allegation that this was all a drunken hallucination experienced by the king[21] fails to explain how the wise men and Daniel were able to read it.[22]

God's choice of a detached hand[23] to deliver this message to Belshazzar is intriguing. In ancient times, casualty counts after a battle were often tabulated by collecting the severed right hands of those KIA. A lifeless, detached hand would then have symbolized "a defeated enemy."[24] Yet the hand that wrote these words did not belong to a defeated, dead god, but a living God of heaven, the God whose very Temple vessels had been transformed into red Solo cups.

Belshazzar's response to the sight of the severed hand is as comical as it is pathetic. His "color changed, and his thoughts alarmed him; his limbs gave way, and his knees knocked together." The phrase "his limbs gave way" is literally "the knots of his loins were loosened (or untied)."[25] To put

---

19. Koldewey, *Excavations of Babylon*, 103.

20. Baldwin notes the Aramaic word used for "lampstand" "is not otherwise known," so it might have been a special lampstand of some kind (*Daniel*, 121).

21. André Lacocque, *The Book of Daniel*, trans. David Pellauer (Atlanta: John Knox, 1979), 94.

22. Longman, *Daniel*, 138.

23. "The vision of a detached hand writing remains one of the most haunting images in literature," (Collins, *Daniel*, 246).

24. John H. Walton, Victor H. Matthews, and Mark W. Chavalas, *The IVP Bible Background Commentary: Old Testament* (Downers Grove, IL: InterVarsity Press, 2000), 737. The authors conclude, "The effect might be similar if the head of a decapitated victim began to speak," (Ibid., 738).

25. Al Wolters, "Untying the King's Knots: Physiology and Wordplay in Daniel 5," *JBL*

it delicately, Belshazzar needed new underwear after he saw the writing on the wall! All together, we are to envision that "a ripple of fear traverses the terrified king's body"[26] (cf. Ps 69:23; Isa 21:3; Jer 50:43; Nah 2:10), and the king began screaming for his wise men to appear.[27]

Why did Belshazzar need interpreters for the writing on the wall? Were the words written in code or a foreign language? The answer might be simpler. The words—abstract, enigmatic nouns—would have been difficult to read (let alone interpret) if they were written in cuneiform or unpointed Aramaic (i.e. all consonants, no vowels).[28] What's more, there may not have been divisions between the words, the consonants just running together. This explanation makes sense. You'd be puzzled too if one day you discovered "dollar, quarter, dime" written on your fancy dining room wall, but with all the vowels missing.

DLLRQRTRDM

That would take you a while to sort out, and then you would have no idea what the phrase meant as a whole. And if you're wondering, the entire scene in Dan 5 strikes me as an ancient version of *Wheel of Fortune* ("I'd like to buy a vowel"), but instead of $30,000 and a trip to Hawaii, you lose your empire at the end of the show.

OK, so maybe you weren't wondering, but there you go.

As his predecessor had done, Belshazzar summoned the wise men and offered a startling promotion to third in the kingdom (he couldn't

---

110 (1991): 117–22. He quotes Walter Cannon, "The involuntary voiding of the bladder and lower gut at times of violent mental stress is well-known," (*Bodily Changes in Pain, Hunger, Fear and Rage* [New York: Appleton, 1916], 33). Wolters also considers the prophecy of Isa 45:1, that Cyrus would "loose the loins of kings" (NASU), to have been directly fulfilled when Belshazzar defecated all over himself.

26. Wolters, "Untying the King's Knots," 117.

27. Miller, *Daniel,* 156.

28. David Instone Brewer, "Mene Mene Teqel Uparsin: Daniel 5:25 in Cuneiform," *TynBul* 42 (1991): 310–16.

offer #2—he was #2, and daddy was #1), along with purple clothes (representing royalty), and a gold chain (cf. Gen 41:42–43; Esth 8:15)—even the Babylonians enjoyed a good piece of bling-bling. But just as Nebuchadnezzar had discovered, the wise men were impotent to explain the message. "By now the reader of the book of Daniel cannot help but picture these men as incompetent fools, and they don't disappoint our expectations."[29] This, too, left the king "greatly alarmed" (5:9).

So in comes the queen—likely Belshazzar's mother;[30] his wives were already present at the party (5:2–3). The queen mother was often a very powerful figure in the ANE[31] (cf. 1 Kgs 1:11–21; 15:13; 2 Kgs 10:13; 11:1–3; 24:12; Jer 13:18; 29:2), so powerful on this occasion that she arrived uninvited (cf. Esth 4:11) and ordered Belshazzar to summon Daniel. She reminded her son of Daniel and praised his service to Nebuchadnezzar; her narrative function is similar to that of Arioch in Dan 2 and the cupbearer in Gen 41. It seems Daniel had not experienced the same favor in Belshazzar's regime as he had in Nebuchadnezzar's. Had Nabonidus or Belshazzar cleaned house of the old advisors and brought in new ones (cf. 1 Kgs 12:8; Prov 25:5), forcing Daniel and his three friends to take an early form of retirement? I think so, for as we are about to see, Daniel had no love lost for Belshazzar as opposed to the warmth he felt for Nebuchadnezzar as evident in the last chapter.

## DANIEL 5:13–23

I can't help but wonder what ran through Daniel's mind as he entered the palace, one that minutes ago had been filled with raucous celebration,

---

29. Longman, *Daniel,* 138–39.

30. There is persuasive evidence that this woman was the famed Nitocris, daughter of Nebuchadnezzar and wife of Nabonidus (Raymond Philip Dougherty, *Nabonidus and Belshazzar* [New Haven, CT: Yale Univ. Press, 1929], 39–42, 51–66, 194). Herodotus eulogized her as possessing extraordinary wisdom (*Histories* 1.185–87).

31. Niels-Erik A. Andreasen, "The Role of the Queen Mother in Israelite Society," *CBQ* 45 (1983): 179–94.

but now possessed all the warmth and frivolity of a funeral home. We aren't told what Daniel thought; I realize that. But he was an aged advisor and prophet. He knew that nearly a century and a half prior, Isaiah had predicted the fall of Babylon (Isa 13, 21), particularly at the hands of a divinely-appointed king named Cyrus (Isa 45:1). He knew Isaiah had foreseen Babylon's humiliation:

> The LORD says, "City of Babylon, go down and sit in the dirt. People of Babylon, sit on the ground. You are no longer the ruler. You will no longer be called tender or beautiful. ... People will see your nakedness; they will see your shame. I will punish you; I will punish every one of you ... Now, listen, you lover of pleasure. You think you are safe. You tell yourself, 'I am the only important person. I will never be a widow or lose my children.' Two things will happen to you suddenly, in a single day. You will lose your children and your husband. These things will truly happen to you, in spite of all your magic, in spite of your powerful tricks. You do evil things, but you feel safe and say, 'No one sees what I do.' Your wisdom and knowledge have fooled you. You say to yourself, 'I am God, and no one is equal to me.' But troubles will come to you, and you will not know how to stop them. Disaster will fall on you, and you will not be able to keep it away. You will be destroyed quickly; you will not even see it coming."
>
> Isa 47:1-11 NCV

Daniel knew this prophecy, and thus he knew ahead of time that the king would summon enchanters and astrologers and wise men, but that they would prove useless.

> Keep on, then, with your magic spells and with your many sorceries, which you have labored at since childhood. Perhaps you will succeed, perhaps you will cause terror.

> All the counsel you have received has only worn you out! Let your astrologers come forward, those stargazers who make predictions month by month, let them save you from what is coming upon you. Surely they are like stubble; the fire will burn them up. They cannot even save themselves from the power of the flame.
>
> Isa 47:12–14 NIV

Daniel knew what was about to happen since, in Belshazzar's first and third years as king, he had received visions predicting the collapse of Babylon and the rise of Persia (Dan 7–8). He had a pretty good idea of why he was being called and what this was all about. He would have witnessed the Persian advance on CNN (the Chaldean News Network). The visions would have informed him the end was near. Before he was summoned, Daniel likely already knew about the handwriting and its message. Daniel would have known its source.

Daniel *knew*.

Upon his entrance, Belshazzar flung a left-handed compliment in Daniel's face; his words to Daniel (5:13–16) are "a complex mixture of skepticism, challenge, desperation, and resentment rather than a 'friendly welcome.'"[32] He seems skeptical of Daniel's aptitude; "Twice he begins his words with 'I have heard.'"[33] "There is a tone of egoism and haughtiness in these words."[34] The king scornfully brought up the fact that Daniel was one of the exiles from Judah, as if this somehow equated the prophet to a country bumpkin and invalidated his many decades of loyal, competent service to the throne. Nevertheless, the king acknowledged Daniel's reputation and offered the same reward to Daniel that had been extended to his failed, fraudulent Magi.

---

32. Fewell, *Circle of Sovereignty*, 94. She speculates that Belshazzar's attitude reflects his jealousy of Nebuchadnezzar's success. In short, "Daniel reminds the king of all that his (grand) father was and all that he is not," (Hill, "Daniel," 109).

33. Longman, *Daniel*, 140.

34. Young, *Daniel*, 123.

But the senior statesman refused. What he was about to say would be difficult to swallow, and he wanted to avoid all appearances that he was in this for the money (cf. 1 Thess 2:4–5). Only after he gave the interpretation did Daniel accept the king's rewards, but Daniel knew the gifts were worthless the moment they were given. Belshazzar might as well have compensated the prophet with Monopoly money.

Daniel reminded the bratty king that Nebuchadnezzar had embodied the totality of Babylon's splendor and enjoyed absolute power over the known world, but that "the Most High God" had given him this splendor and power (5:18). When his pride had become too much, Nebuchadnezzar had been punished by God "until he knew that the Most High God rules the kingdom of mankind and sets over it whom he will" (5:21).

Though Belshazzar was acquainted with this well-known event, he had not taken it to heart. "Belshazzar is condemned precisely because the example he might have followed was so close to him that it removed all possible excuse."[35] Instead, he had been foolish enough to lift himself up "against the Lord of heaven" (5:23) and effectively spit in his eye. On the eve of his demise, Belshazzar had decided to appeal to the gods of gold, silver, bronze, iron, wood, and stone—gods that could not help him. "But the God in whose hand is your breath, and whose are all your ways, you have not honored" (5:23; cf. Job 12:10; Ps 104:29; Acts 17:28).

"The old prophet's words demonstrated great courage in the face of a monarch who held the power of life and death over him."[36] Like Nathan (2 Sam 12), Elijah (1 Kgs 21), and Jeremiah (Jer 38) before him, Daniel stood in the presence of a king to bring a word of judgment from a more powerful King. Things were about to get interesting.

## DANIEL 5:24–31

In explaining the handwriting to the king, Daniel read the words as

35. Anderson, *Signs and Wonders*, 53.

36. Miller, *Daniel*, 164.

nouns (i.e. monetary weights),[37] but interpreted them as verbs. This is the meaning of the mysterious inscription:

***Mene, Mene***: "God has numbered the days of your kingdom and brought it to an end" (5:26). As a noun, the term stood for a mina; as a verb, the word means "to number." It is mentioned twice since it has a double meaning—"to count" and "to fix the limit of."[38] Because God is sovereign, knowing the end from the beginning (Isa 46:10), he has fixed the days of every empire and ruler. No one reigns indefinitely.

***Tekel***: "You have been weighed in the balances and found wanting" (5:27; cf. 1 Sam 2:3; Job 31:6; Prov 16:2). Tekel or "shekel" was 1/60th of a mina; the verb form meant "to weigh." Like Sodom, the moral state of Babylon had reached a level God would no longer tolerate. Their sins had reached their full measure (Gen 15:16). Scripture testifies that, while God judges the individual in the hereafter, he judges nations in the here-and-now. Just as he judged Babylon, Rome, Nazi Germany, and the Soviet Union, he will also judge America one day, and all other nations that rise and fall until the end of time.

***Parsin***: Daniel reinterprets the final word as Peres, which is often considered a pun on "Persia."[39] "Your kingdom is divided and given to the Medes and Persians" (5:28). The noun meant a half-shekel; the verb meant "to divide." It was God's sovereign good pleasure to do with Babylon as he willed; it is no different today. "Many are the plans in a person's heart, but it is the LORD's purpose that prevails" (Prov 19:21 NIV).

If there is only one thing commendable about Belshazzar's behavior in this chapter, it's that he kept his word after an unfavorable interpretation was given.[40] He clothed Daniel in purple, brought him the bling-bling, and proclaimed him third-most-powerful in the empire. The prophet

37. Emil G. Kraeling, "The Handwriting on the Wall," *JBL* 63 (1944): 11–18.

38. Leupold, *Daniel*, 234. Miller says Mene is repeated "to stress that the divine decision was certain of fulfillment," (*Daniel*, 165).

39. Hill, "Daniel," 112.

40. Lucas believes he was only saving face in front of his nobles (*Daniel*, 134).

was now ethically free to accept the reward since he had delivered an unfavorable interpretation. Daniel was clearly not for sale; he knew the rewards were meaningless anyway for "that very night," the Medes and Persians captured Babylon.

The Greek historians Herodotus and Xenophon confirm the biblical record. Herodotus says Cyrus captured the city (but did not destroy it) by redirecting the flow of the Euphrates, and his troops waded along the waterless riverbed where it passed under the city walls. Xenophon records how Cyrus' generals came upon Belshazzar with a dagger in hand, attempting suicide, but they "overpowered him" and executed him (*Cyropaedia* 7.5.29–30, 32). They both note that these events took place on a night when seemingly all Babylon was having a party (*Histories* 1.191; *Cyropaedia* 7.5.15).

Secular history may record that Babylon fell that night because she was bested by a better empire. But just as God had given Jerusalem into Nebuchadnezzar's hand, he now gave Babylon into Cyrus'. More specifically, God brought judgment upon Belshazzar because he had dared to mock the Most High.[41] At that point, one imagines a cute little girl on a tricycle could have brought about the demise of this king had it been God's will to use her as his agent. But as God would have it, the mighty empire of Babylon vanished in a night without even so much as a prolonged siege.[42] Just as Jeremiah predicted, she sank like a rock to the bottom of history's river "to rise no more" (Jer 51:64; cf. Isa 13).

Behold, the derision of heaven.

---

41. "Judgment in history falls heaviest on those who come to think themselves gods, who fly in the face of Providence and history, who put their trust in man-made systems and worship the work of their own hands, and who say that the strength of their own right arm gave them the victory," (H. Butterfield, *Christianity and History* [New York: Scribner's, 1950], 60).

42. Both Herodotus (*Histories* 1.190) and Xenophon (*Cyropaedia* 7.5.13) claim Babylon could have endured a siege of twenty years with their massive stockpile of provisions.

ONE FINAL NOTE—throughout the party, Belshazzar drank heavily. I wonder, with all the alcohol he consumed, did it really register how much he offered as a reward, first to the wise men, then to Daniel, in exchange for an interpretation of this mysterious writing? Even as he summoned the purple robe and gold chain for Daniel, he may well have been plastered beyond his senses. Was it the dirty cocktail of arrogance and alcohol that prevented him from humbly praising Daniel's God as Nebuchadnezzar had done in each of the three previous episodes? When the Persian military executed him that night, was Belshazzar in full control of his faculties—in his "right mind" as Nebuchadnezzar had been at the end of Dan 4?

One does not have to be literally drunk to miss the many opportunities God affords us to reconcile our relationship with him, to enthrone him in our hearts. All that is required to "miss it" is a heart obsessed with temporary things on earth and not eternal ones in heaven. But the moment we awake from our drunken slumber—the moment we say "Yes!" to God and "No!" to the world's darkness—that's when true life begins!

"Wake up, sleeper, rise from the dead, and Christ will shine on you" (Eph 5:14 NIV).

## TALKING POINTS

IMPATIENCE IS A GREAT enemy of my ministry. In a world of blazing download speeds, I have foolishly thought one sermon or counseling session could fix whatever was wrong in churches and people. When change didn't happen overnight, my reaction was a toxic mixture of despondency and cynicism, but neither has any place in the heart of God's servant. Paul exhorted Timothy to "preach the word ... with complete patience" (2 Tim 4:2). I wonder how Daniel felt as he witnessed all the progress made with Nebuchadnezzar go up in the smoke of an insolent, bratty king like Belshazzar. Perhaps his perspective, one that spanned nearly seventy years, reminded him that faithfulness was more important than immediate progress. In God's way of working, progress and success often occur so slowly that they are unobservable. Seeds planted can take decades or centuries to yield a harvest. "One can never realize fully the leavening influence faithful lives can have on the world."[43] Christian, never forget that as you labor in God's kingdom! He does not call you to be the most successful or fruitful, but to trust him completely in all things. If you can cultivate a heart that seeks faithfulness, not flash, you will enjoy Daniel's longevity in service to your King (cf. 1 Cor 15:58; Gal 6:9; Phil 1:6).

BELSHAZZAR SHOULD have learned from the mistakes of Nebuchadnezzar, but he neglected the warning and spurned God's mercy. The Lord is patient with us, giving us many opportunities to turn to him to be saved from coming destruction (2 Pet 3:9). It is nothing short of a witness to his grace that he does not take our lives the first time we sin—that is surely what we deserve. "Little do people realize that every breath they take is only because of God's grace."[44] We are no different than Belshazzar; we too have polluted what God considers holy (cf. 1 Cor 6:19–20). How

43. Hailey, *Daniel*, 106.

44. Wood, *Daniel*, 148.

many occasions have you intentionally disobeyed your heavenly Father, yet he did not strip you of life "that very night" as he did Belshazzar? Perhaps, in the back of your mind, you have been silencing the voice warning you of the need to be reconciled to God, but you ignore this voice, planning to make things right when it's more convenient. How many more chances will you receive before your sins reach their limit, your time runs out, and God has had enough? Two? A hundred? A thousand? "Or do you presume on the riches of his kindness and forbearance and patience, not knowing that God's kindness is meant to lead you to repentance?" (Rom 2:4).

Reflecting on Dan 5, Boice wrote, "The only thing more certain for us than death and taxes is the final judgment."[45] For us, "the writing is on the wall," and it is not as mysterious or enigmatic as that given to Belshazzar. On the final day, God will judge all people according to their deeds (Rev 20:13). Indeed, "there's a sad day coming ... when the sinner shall hear his doom, 'Depart, I know ye not.'" But this does not have to be your fate, friend! In Christ, the written record against us is nullified (Col 2:14). In Christ, we don't stand condemned (Rom 8:1)! "Seek then, Beloved, to be united unto Christ by faith; and then, instead of trembling at his approach, you shall 'rejoice before him at his coming.'"[46] God's wrath is a righteous, yet terrible thing. Do not waste another moment of your life; don't wait a second longer, or it might be too late! Jesus is the only refuge from the wrath of God (Rom 5:9). "Kiss the Son, lest he be angry, and you perish in the way, for his wrath is quickly kindled. Blessed are all who take refuge in him" (Ps 2:12). Only in Jesus can you escape the derision and judgment of a righteous God!

45. Boice, *Daniel*, 67.

46. Charles Simeon, *Expository Outlines on the Whole Bible*, vol. 9 (Grand Rapids: Zondervan, 1956), 495.

# 6

# THE LION KING

I suppose Daniel and lions go together like peanut butter and jelly. When you think of the biblical Daniel, this story comes to mind. My dad always titled his column in the church bulletin or local newspaper "Daniel's Den." When my son, Daniel Isaac, was born, someone gave him a stuffed lion as a gift. A popular kid's song goes "Daniel, Daniel, Daniel, Daniel, Daniel in the li- li- lions' ... den." Maybe because "Daniel and the shiny statue" or "Daniel and the chopped down tree" isn't as engaging.

In *The Epic of God*, I discussed how Noah's Flood has lost a large degree of its awfulness and tragedy by being transformed into a lovable children's tale.[1] I wonder if the same hasn't happened for this story in Dan 6. We turn the lions into cuddly kitty cats that pose no threat. But the danger of this story was real and should not be passed over too quickly. As I mentioned in chapter 3, our proclivity is to handle gruesome OT stories with delicacy, and we more or less limit them to children's classes in our churches.

To contemplate a night in a den of lions is, well, beyond terrifying. I remember the first time I watched *Jurassic Park* and saw the tyrannosaurus tear various people limb from limb. Gruesome? Yes, but no more than this story. Instead of robotic or CGI dinosaurs, real lions threatened to maim, then eat, a human being.

The annals of God's martyrs are filled with similar stories, ones that

---

1. Michael Whitworth, *The Epic of God* (Bowie, TX: Start2Finish Books, 2012), 61.

actually came to pass because God in his wisdom chose *not* to deliver his saints from suffering. As was the case with the episode in Dan 3, these stories are not intended to give us the false hope that God will deliver us from every trial, but that he is present with us in our suffering, and that nothing can separate us from his love (Rom 8:38–39). The apostle Paul knew God had preserved his life on countless occasions (2 Cor 11:23–28) because Paul's ministry wasn't yet complete. But there came a day when Rome's executioner laid the axe on the apostle's neck. Only then did God bring him "safely into his heavenly kingdom" (2 Tim 4:18).

In that light, Paul Lederach warns, "In telling these stories today, the church must exercise caution lest the relationship with God is reduced to a triumphal, commercial transaction: if you do this, then God will do that! ... When God intervenes, it is to accomplish his purposes, not ours."[2] The point of these stories is not to expect God's miraculous intervention, but to demonstrate to God's people that he is present with those willing to suffer death rather than betray their allegiance to and reliance on the God of heaven. "God calls some to win by living. Others are called to win by dying. But in life or death God rules and we are called to serve him."[3]

In Dan 3, Daniel's three friends refused to break the first two commandments, even if it meant death. Theirs was a refusal to do something they knew was wrong. Here, Daniel refused to *cease* doing something he knew to be right, even if it meant death (cf. Jas 4:17). The call to faithfulness demands we say *No!* to some things while maintaining an eager *Yes!* to others. Through it all, we are confident that God is with us until he brings us safely into his heavenly kingdom.

## DARIUS THE MEDE

At the end of Dan 5, we're told "Darius the Mede received the kingdom, being about sixty-two years old" (5:31), and this same Darius is

2. Paul M. Lederach, *Daniel* (Scottdale, PA: Herald Press, 1994), 144.

3. Boice, *Daniel*, 78.

a main character in Dan 6. Very simply, we aren't exactly sure who Darius was, but it seems certain he was not the same as Darius I (522–486 B.C.), who was under thirty when he assumed the throne. If these two were one in the same, Daniel would have been approaching 100 years of age when the lions' den narrative took place.

Because identifying Darius with any historical person has proven so difficult, some scholars have alleged he was a fictional character. Others have identified the Darius of Daniel with Darius I and then claimed the author of Daniel flunked out of History 101.[4] But those who believe the Bible to be from God (and thus historically accurate) must categorically reject such a notion. Convinced that Darius was a historical figure, and that the inspired writer was not mistaken, here are the two best options proposed so far:

***Darius was another name for Cyrus the Great.*** Wiseman first asserted this in 1956. According to all historical records, including the Bible (2 Chr 36:22–23; Ezra 1:1–8; Isa 45:1), Cyrus conquered Babylon in 539 and allowed the exiles to return to Jerusalem. In Daniel, it is said "Darius the Mede" was 62 when Babylon was conquered; Cyrus was the same age when he conquered Babylon, and he seems to have gone by the title "king of the Medes" while in Babylon.[5] In Dan 11:1, the LXX reads "Cyrus," not "Darius," suggesting the LXX translators knew of the double name. The final verse of Dan 1 says Daniel served "until the first year of King Cyrus."

The best argument, however, may boil down to how one translates "and" in 6:28. The word "and" in Semitic languages such as Hebrew and Aramaic can serve an explanatory function, not just conjunctive; the

4. "The claim of the book of Daniel to be a work of history, written by a well-informed contemporary, is shattered beyond repair by this fiction of Darius the Mede," (H. H. Rowley, *Darius the Mede and the Four World Empires of the Book of Daniel* [Cardiff: Univ. of Wales Press Board, 1935], 59).

5. Donald J. Wiseman, "The Last Days of Babylon," *Christianity Today*, Nov 25, 1957, 10. Archer says "Darius" may have been a throne name deriving from a Persian word meaning "king" and similar in function to "Caesar" for the Romans ("Daniel," 76–77; cf. Wood, *Daniel*, 155).

Greek *kai* also functions in this way (e.g. Matt 8:33; 21:5).[6] Baker cites 1 Sam 17:40 and Dan 4:10, as well as a 5th century B.C. loan contract, as examples of "and" serving an explanatory role.[7] Another example would be 1 Chr 5:26, where "Pul king of Assyria" is equated with "Tiglath-pileser king of Assyria" since they were the same person. To summarize, then, the best way to translate 6:28 would be "Daniel prospered during the reign of Darius, *that is* the reign of Cyrus the Persian."[8]

***Darius was another name for Gubaru*** (known in Greek texts as Gobryas), Cyrus' governor over Babylon and all lands west of the Euphrates for about fourteen years, meaning he ruled beyond Cyrus' death. That he was appointed ruler of the region would harmonize with the statement that Darius was "made king over the realm of the Chaldeans" (9:1) as if by a higher authority.[9] The statement in 6:28 would then mean Darius (i.e. Gubaru) and Cyrus ruled concurrently. Whitcomb postulated this view in 1959.[10] From cuneiform texts, it does seem Gubaru cast an imposing, king-like shadow over his subjects.[11] But the problem with this

6. William Arndt, Frederick W. Danker, and Walter Bauer, *A Greek-English Lexicon of the New Testament and Other Early Christian Literature,* 3rd ed. (Chicago: Univ. of Chicago Press, 2000), 495.

7. David W. Baker, "Further Examples of the Waw Explicativum," *VT* 30 (1980): 129–36. He concludes, "This function of the conjunction is not rare. It occurs throughout the Old Testament in all the classical source documents and in various literary genres. Not only is this a phenomenon of Biblical Hebrew, it also occurs in other North-West and East Semitic languages," (Ibid., 134).

8. For more discussion that identifies Darius with Cyrus, see Miller, *Daniel,* 174–77.

9. That this Darius "received the kingdom" (5:31) and "was made king" (9:1), as if by a superior, is Archer's argument against identifying Darius with Cyrus, who took the Babylonian Empire by force. "Who could have appointed Cyrus king when he himself was already the supreme authority in the entire Middle East?" (Archer, "Daniel," 18). But I find this argument unpersuasive since the book of Daniel emphatically declares that the God of heaven gives kingdoms to whomever he pleases (2:21; 5:21).

10. John C. Whitcomb, Jr., *Darius the Mede* (Grand Rapids: Eerdmans, 1959).

11. Whitcomb calls Gubaru the "*de facto* king of Babylon" (Ibid., 33), and Olmstead concludes Gubaru "ruled almost as an independent monarch," (A. T. Olmstead, *History of the Persian Empire* [Chicago: Univ. of Chicago Press, 1948], 56).

view is there is "no specific evidence that he [Gubaru] was a Mede, called king, named Darius, a son of Ahasuerus, or aged about 60."[12]

I personally consider Wiseman's suggestion to be the best, though I must stress again that we can't be completely sure. However, bear in mind that for so many centuries, there was not a single mention of Belshazzar outside of Scripture. For that reason, critics accused the Bible of being fallible. Now, they have no such claim in regards to Belshazzar. "There is no real reason for doubting the historical reliability of this or any other biblical book."[13] It is generational arrogance to assume that, if something has not yet been discovered or validated in our day, it must not be true. But who's to say that, somewhere in Mesopotamia, we might one day discover some artifact that settles the Darius debate once and for all?

## DANIEL 6:1–9

The Medo-Persian Empire was the largest the world had seen at that time. It stretched from India to Ethiopia and, during the time of Esther, was composed of 127 satrapies (Esth 1:1; 8:9)—*satrap* meant "protector of the empire."[14] In the time of Daniel, the number was 120 (6:1). Over these 120 satraps were three "administrators" (HCSB) or "commissioners" (NASU), similar to the seven princes/counselors under Xerxes (Esth 1:14) and Artaxerxes (Ezra 7:14).

Part of Daniel's responsibilities as one of the commissioners was to prevent military revolts and oversee the collection of tax revenue for the king and ensure that he was not cheated (cf. Ezra 4:13, 22). This obviously was a position reserved for only those men with the highest integrity. Daniel had been a favored advisor in the court of Nebuchadnezzar; now he was rising in the ranks of a second empire. Daniel even began to

---

12. D. J. Wiseman, "Darius" in *New Bible Dictionary*, 3rd ed. (Downers Grove, IL: InterVarsity Press, 1996), 257. Against these detractions, see Whitcomb, *Darius the Mede*, 28–42.

13. Boice, *Daniel*, 73.

14. HALOT 5:1811.

distinguish himself over the other two administrators to the point that "the king planned to set him over the whole kingdom" (6:3).

Out of envy, the other two administrators and several of the satraps plotted to ruin Daniel.[15] They sought for cause to have him dismissed or worse, but their search was fruitless. Daniel "was faithful, and no error or fault was found in him" (6:4; cf. 1 Pet 2:12). They likely wanted to malign Daniel as being dishonest with money or causing trouble, but he was beyond reproach.[16] Daniel was so filled with integrity that they decided the only way to get rid of him was to pit his allegiance to God vs. his allegiance to king and country. So they conspired (cf. Ps 2:1) and made a proposal to Darius that no one be allowed to pray for a month to any man or god except Darius. The punishment for the disobedience was being cast into the lions' den (6:7).[17] The entire plot hinged on two things: Daniel's faithfulness to his God and the well-attested irrevocability of "the law of the Medes and the Persians" (6:8, 12, 15; cf. Esth 1:19; 8:8).[18]

If Darius and Cyrus were one in the same, this decree would have made sense politically. This move would have consolidated loyalty to the new regime that had recently deposed Nabonidus and Belshazzar. But several scholars have struggled with the idea of a Persian king deifying himself since we have no other record of this ever happening. Walton therefore suggests the decree, in effect, did not deify the king, but rather designated

15. "The devil stirs the fires of natural hatred to a fiercer heat as soon as God's children are involved," (Leupold, *Daniel*, 251).

16. "An honest man of conviction in the midst of government or ecclesiastical politicians stands out like a fair flower in a barren wilderness," (Young, *Daniel*, 133).

17. The word translated "den" simply means "pit," so the lions' den in this story was likely a large, underground space similar to a cave with a hole at the top (to feed the lions) that could be sealed with a stone (Lucas, *Daniel*, 150).

18. The Code of Hammurabi levied a penalty on any judge that altered his sentence (§5). According to the Greek historian Diodorus Siculus, Darius III (336-330 B.C.) once sentenced an innocent man to death, but couldn't rescind the order since the law was irrevocable (*Histories* 17.30).

him "as the only legitimate representative of deity for the stated time."[19] Hailey explains that Darius benevolently wanted to become familiar with the religious views and petitions of his subjects; receiving these "prayer requests" for a month would place Darius "in a better position to govern as their king."[20]

Whatever the exact nature of the decree, the point is that Daniel's enemies intended to use it to trap Daniel and bring about his demise. The same thing happens today in every system of government—evil individuals use a complex system of laws to harm the people of God and hide their subsequent guilt. "It is much easier on our conscience if we can blame the system."[21] It was law that was appealed to when Jesus was sentenced to die (John 19:7). But the God of Daniel sees all wickedness and has assured us he will "bring every deed into judgment, including every hidden thing, whether it is good or evil" (Eccl 12:14 NIV).

## DANIEL 6:10–18

Once the decree had been made, Daniel had several options. Obviously, he could have ceased praying for the month. The decree was not indefinite; surely God would understand if one of his favorite people ever (cf. Ezek 14:14, 20) took the month off. He could have also found a more private place to pray other than his upper room—like, say, his tornado shelter or safe room. Nowhere in Scripture are we required to pray at an open window facing Jerusalem. What was to keep Daniel from following Jesus' teaching about going into an inner room, shutting the door, and praying in secret (Matt 6:6)? Neither option was a good one; Daniel could not cease what he had been doing. Darius twice praised Daniel for serving his God "continually" (6:16, 20), and "given that his piety was

19. John H. Walton, "The Decree of Darius the Mede in Daniel 6," *JETS* 31 (1988): 280. He rightly argues that for the king to have completely prohibited prayer, even for a month, would have been "unenforceable and politically suicidal," (Ibid., 282).

20. Hailey, *Daniel*, 113–14.

21. Wallace, *The Lord Is King*, 111.

apparently well-known, to do so would have been to compromise."[22] We may be tempted at times to "scale back" because to do otherwise would make things difficult for us. God may understand our "temporary retreat," for he remembers that we are dust, that we are frail (Ps 103:14). But doing so would not be consistent with what it means to live by faith (2 Cor 5:7), and "without faith no one can please God" (Heb 11:6 NCV). "Any gain made at the price of faithfulness to God's word proves ultimately to be loss" (cf. Phil 3:7–8).[23]

Instead of taking the month off or scaling back his outward display of inward devotion, Daniel continued to do what "he had done previously" (6:10). "This was no sporadic act of bravado. It was a regular and disciplined exercise by means of which he practised the presence of God."[24] Take note, friend: Daniel preferred to face the lions than go a month without praying. Can the same be said for us? Daniel's habit included three daily prayers (cf. Ps 55:17) on his knees[25] in his "upper chamber." "This was not an attic but a room on the flat roof of the house. These rooms were, and still are, common in the East, being used as private apartments to which one retired when wishing to be undisturbed. They usually had latticed windows which allowed free circulation of air."[26]

That Daniel prayed with his face in the direction of Jerusalem indicates not only his piety, but also his commitment to spiritual revival

---

22. Lucas, *Daniel*, 154.

23. Sinclair B. Ferguson, "Daniel," in *New Bible Commentary*, 4th ed. (Downers Grove, IL: InterVarsity Press, 1994), 755.

24. Russell, *Daniel*, 102. "Observe, it is not said that he opened his windows; it is quite the contrary, 'His windows being open;'—to shut them now would be cowardice; whereas to have opened them, if he had previously been in the habit of keeping them closed, would have been to court persecution,—a foolhardy thing, which the child of God is never called upon to do," (Ironside, *Daniel*, 102).

25. "Kneeling is the posture in which a person is the most 'defenseless,' and in prayer it is a symbol of dependence, humility, and contrition before God," (Hill, "Daniel," 122).

26. Judah J. Slotki, *Ezra-Nehemiah-Daniel* (London: Soncino, 1951), 49.

among the Jews (cf. 1 Kgs 8:35–36).[27] This seems to have been a common practice during the exile (1 Esdras 4:58). It necessitated spiritual eyes to see the value of such an endeavor. "The fact that Jerusalem was in ruins called forth faith that it would again be restored because the God who had set his name on the city was the continuing, unchanging God, in control of history."[28] That same God who controlled history also controlled Daniel's future. Daniel knew there would be problems related to the new decree, and that's why prayer was his first recourse.

At this point in his life, Daniel was in his eighties, and prayer had become a primary means of dealing with times of stress and trial. What possible reason did he have to stop now? With each passing day, I too believe more and more in the power of prayer. Too often, we regard this weapon as a last resort, something to which we turn when we've exhausted every other option—"All we can do now is pray"—as if we could do anything greater? Especially in times of crisis and persecution, Christians' greatest weapon against tyranny and oppression is not the use of force or the consolidation of political clout, but prayer (e.g. Acts 12:12). Indeed, prayer is more subversive to earthly authority than rebellion, for rebellion acknowledges the power of the state, while prayer appeals to a higher power whose ultimate will cannot be thwarted.[29] As we will see later, for Christians to respond to threats in fleshly ways is to declare that our struggle is *not* "against the spiritual forces of evil in the heavenly realms" (Eph 6:12 NIV). But Daniel knew better, and that's why Daniel prayed "as he had done previously" (6:10).

Daniel's enemies were waiting on him to violate the law, and I imagine they did not have to wait long. They quickly informed the king of Daniels' disobedience, painting him as one all too eager to scorn the king

---

27. "Even though this shekinah cloud had forsaken the temple prior to the Fall of Jerusalem in 587 (Ezek 11:23), Daniel knew that the Lord had promised to return there (cf. Ezek 43:2)," (Archer, "Daniel," 80).

28. Baldwin, *Daniel*, 129.

29. Walter Wink, *Naming the Powers* (Philadelphia: Fortress, 1984), 110–11.

and the decree. They insinuated to Darius that Daniel's insubordinate act made him a dangerous subversive.[30] "These enemies of Daniel must have thought at that juncture of affairs that they had everything under control. They overlooked the *will of God*, which is a universal characteristic of all wicked men."[31]

Yet Darius obviously knew better than to buy into this notion that Daniel was a rebel. The king "was much distressed" when he heard this and spent the rest of the day[32] seeking a way out of the dilemma. He knew Daniel was a faithful servant to the empire; he knew Daniel's dedication to king and country was only surpassed by his dedication to God. It's possible Darius was attempting an official investigation or formal trial of Daniel to delay or prevent the execution. But his effort to find a loophole failed, and I believe God was behind this failure. "Had it been found, the story would have lost both its point and its poignancy."[33]

In this scene, Darius is to be pitied. "There is irony in the fact that the king who sought to portray himself as the one through whom everyone's petitions could be answered finds that he cannot bring about the one thing that he wants to happen."[34] The sovereign ruler over so great an empire wasn't so sovereign anymore. He knew he was a victim of his own law and his own civil servants (cf. Prov 29:20; Matt 14:9).[35] The king's anguish is palpable in the text, but he had no choice.[36] Daniel was summoned and thrown into the den of lions.

---

30. Hill, "Daniel," 121.

31. Coffman, *Daniel*, 100.

32. "The execution of the sentence was carried out, according to Oriental custom, on the evening of the day in which the accusation was made," (Keil, *Daniel*, 215).

33. Anderson, *Signs and Wonders*, 70.

34. Lucas, *Daniel*, 151.

35. "Kings are the slaves of their flatterers," (Jamieson, *Commentary*, 4:414).

36. Reflecting on Darius' dilemma, Maclaren exhorts, "Therefore let us take heed of the quality of actions and motives, since we are wholly incapable of estimating the sweep of their consequences," (*Expositions*, 78).

Before the opening to the den was sealed, Darius encouraged Daniel: "May your God, whom you serve continually, deliver you!" (6:16).[37] So great had Daniel's witness been in the court of the king that Darius believed it possible his favorite employee would indeed survive the night by the power of God. Then the opening to the den was closed with a stone, and both the king and Daniel's enemies sealed it with their signet rings (cf. Matt 27:66). "The king could not open the den and deliver Daniel, neither could the satraps kill him and the other party not know it."[38] Throughout the night, the king fasted and couldn't sleep.[39] No sleep aids were brought to Darius—no Ambien, no milk, no counting sheep, no reading of the royal records, no dancing girls, no concubines, no music, no sound machine, and none of my dad's sermons on tape.

Meanwhile, as the king suffered from insomnia, how did Daniel spend the night? In prayer to God, petitioning his protection and then thanking him for the answered prayer? Did he, in complete trust, snuggle up to a lion and "and sleep as soundly as if in his bed at home?"[40] Did Daniel and the angel microwave popcorn and watch *The Lion King* at the insistence of their, umm, "hosts"? One wonders…

## DANIEL 6:19–28

A new day had scarcely dawned when Darius beat a path back to the lions' den (cf. Matt 28:1). "O Daniel, servant of the living God, has your God, whom you serve continually, been able to deliver you from the lions?" (6:20).

37. "Interestingly, the king complies with his own law in having Daniel thrown into the lions' pit (v. 16a) but then violates his own edict by invoking the name of Daniel's God in his petition that his choice servant be delivered (v. 16b)," (Hill, "Daniel," 122).

38. Hailey, *Daniel*, 118. "Ironically, these precautions served the divine purpose most wonderfully," (Myers, *Daniel*, 204).

39. "His helplessness suggests to us that it is better to be a child of faith in a den of lions than a king in a palace without faith," (Ferguson, *Daniel*, 140).

40. Hailey, *Daniel*, 118.

Pause. Ponder those tense seconds between Darius' question and Daniel's answer. On trial here was the power of God to deliver his most faithful servant from the fangs of frightening beasts. Had God been faithful? Successful? Was Daniel still alive? Don't rush past this scene without contemplating how anxious and out-of-breath Darius must have been to know the answer—to know if Daniels' God had delivered.

I want you to appreciate the tension that exists between "God can" and "God will." We live our lives within that tension. We know God can do something about our suffering, but will he? In this tense area of in-between is where Satan thrives. In this soil, he plants seeds of doubt in our hearts and nurtures them until they have borne the ugly fruit of indignation, rebellion, and death. But there is something we can place in that gap to frustrate Satan's schemes—not faith in God's deliverance, for he does not always do so, but confidence that God will do what's ultimately best for us. God always does whatever will bring him glory, and God glorifying himself is what is ultimately best for us.

To the king's inquiry, Daniel replied that God had indeed delivered him. An angel had been sent to shut the lions' mouths (Heb 11:33). Daniel's deliverance was due to the power of God and to his being "found blameless"[41] in his service to God and to Darius. Our being blameless does not mean we earn God's protection, for such is always by his grace. Nor will God deliver us out of every crisis alive, but we know he shows favor on those who obey him. When Daniel was lifted out of the den, "no wound was found on him, because he had trusted in his God" (6:23 NIV).

No sooner was Daniel back in the land of the living than those "who had maliciously accused" him[42] were thrown into the den *along with their families* (cf. Prov 11:8; 26:27). In the ANE, anyone bringing a false charge

41. Surviving a threatening ordeal was often considered proof of innocence in the ANE (cf. Num 5:11–31; Longman, *Daniel*, 163). "Blameless" in 6:22 (cf. "innocent," NIV) "is a legal term, probably borrowed from Akkadian," (Lucas, *Daniel*, 144), meaning Daniel was formally acquitted of all charges after surviving the lions' den (cf. 1 Macc 2:60).

42. The LXX has only the two administrators and their families being thrown into the den.

against someone was punished in like manner (cf. Deut 19:16–21; Prov 19:5, 9; 21:28; Esth 7:10). Or as Proverbs puts it: "Lead good people down a wrong path and you'll come to a bad end" (28:10 Msg). Daniel's enemies had incited the derision of heaven and were now made to drink the cup of God's wrath. To throw the families to the lions along with the men seems rather severe to our modern minds, "but it reflects the principle of corporate solidarity that was so common in the biblical world"[43] (Josh 7:24–26; Esth 9:24–25; cf. Deut 24:16). As a parallel, Herodotus says Darius I once executed a high-ranking official name Intaphrenes, along with his entire family, when he was declared guilty of orchestrating a coup (*Histories* 3.119).

As Daniel was lifted out of the den, Josephus claims his enemies cried foul by alleging the lions had been previously fed and had not harmed Daniel since their bellies were full. Darius then threw meat into the den, and after the lions had had their fill, he tossed in Daniel's enemies and their families. "It appeared plain to Darius, after the princes had been cast to the wild beasts, that it was God who preserved Daniel, for the lions spared none of them, but tore them all to pieces, as if they had been very hungry and wanted food," (*Antiquities* 10.260–62).

As Nebuchadnezzar had done in Dan 4, Darius sent a letter—a new decree—to the nations. Many of the theological themes of Daniel are echoed here: God is eternal, as is his kingdom, and he has the absolute power to save and work miracles at will.

If their artwork is any indicator, early Christians considered Daniel's survival of the lions' den to be a shadow of Jesus' death, burial, and resurrection. There are several parallels between the stories—both were falsely accused and brought to trial before powerful rulers seemingly reluctant to hand down a death sentence. Both were sealed in

43. Robert B. Chisholm, Jr., *Handbook on the Prophets* (Grand Rapids: Baker, 2002), 303.

their "graves" with a large stone and signet rings; both had visitors come to their "graves" early in the morning; when both emerged from their "graves," their enemies were humiliated. But the stories diverge on one single point. Daniel was not abandoned in the lions' den, but Jesus was abandoned on the cross (Matt 27:46; cf. 2 Cor 5:21; Heb 13:12). In both cases, it was God's sovereign will to do so; he used the wickedness of man to our advantage (Acts 2:23). God's presence with Daniel in the lions' den reminds us he will not forsake us in our suffering, but God's abandonment of his special Son on the cross reminds us he will not forsake us in our *sin*.

Priorities matter, so God's people must never forget that sin is our greatest problem and Satan our greatest enemy. Not cancer. Not the economy. Not socialism. Sin and Satan. Through being forsaken by God, Jesus can now offer us mercy and forgiveness by blotting out our debt, even though we're the ones who placed him in the "lions' den"! And it is not from the wrath of the lions that Jesus saves us, but from the wrath of God (Rom 5:9). Let's keep that in mind as we venture forth into a unknown future. We shouldn't be known as Republicans or Democrats, Tea Party conservatives or social liberals. The world's most pressing need is not a better government or a stronger economy, but a Savior. Christ "is our only hope for glory" (Col 1:27 NCV). This should be our only message to the world so that everyone, like Daniel, can be declared blameless on the day of Christ (1 Cor 1:8; Col 1:28).

## TALKING POINTS

THE PLOT OF Daniel's enemies was perfectly schemed. Their appeal was to the ego of an emperor—foolproof! But their plan was also dependent upon Daniel's absolute dedication to the Lord. Put another way, if Daniel's faith failed him, so would the plot of his enemies. It is remarkable to think that they trusted Daniel to be faithful. "These people calculated upon Daniel, and they had a right to calculate upon him. Could the world calculate upon us, that we would rather go to the lions' den than conform to what God and our consciences told us to be a sin? If not, we have not yet learned what it means to be a disciple."[44] The world watches us even as it accuses us (1 Pet 2:12). To be a Christian requires carrying a cross and dying daily; it requires that we seek first Jesus' kingdom rather than an earthly one (Matt 6:33). Being a follower of Jesus means we embrace inevitable persecution (2 Tim 3:12). When we betray our values in the face of adversity and do things we know to be wrong—or worse, cease doing things we know are right—we espouse a terrible witness to the world.

THOUGH WE MIGHT, in a fit of patriotism, declare the U.S. to be the best country on earth, there are two words that mitigate my enthusiasm: *on earth*. Part of the problem with earthly rulers is they must concern themselves with public opinion, and the masses are often wrong. Whether we prefer democracies (majority rules), republics (elected representatives listening to the cacophony of the people), or autocracies (easily-corrupted, dictatorial madmen), government will always disappoint us if we depend on it (Jer 17:5). It's the consequence of living in a fallen world, and it's why we should swear our greatest allegiance to King Jesus and claim citizenship in heaven (Phil 3:20). Darius is by far the most amenable monarch in the book of Daniel, but even he was powerless to rescue Daniel from danger—any faith in Darius was misplaced. The same could

44. Maclaren, *Expositions*, 75.

be said for the U.S. Constitution and the concept of the rule of law. Both are good things, but trusting in them is foolish. The NT calls us to pray for our political leaders, to honor them, and to obey the law as long as doing so doesn't violate God's law. But *our faith is always to be in Christ* since such a faith guards us (Eph 6:16; 1 Pet 1:5) and thereby overcomes the world (1 John 5:4). All political leaders will disappoint us, Republicans and Democrats alike; even the Constitution is imperfect. Our energy is better spent trusting and worshiping the Lord Jesus Christ (Ps 2:12).

Fabian von Schlabrendorf, a lawyer in Nazi Germany who wasn't particularly religious, was tortured for his opposition to Hitler. Reflecting on that experience, he later said, "Those of us who had never learned to pray did so now, and found that prayer, and only prayer, can bring comfort in such terrible straits."[45] The NT command to pray, and to do so "without ceasing" (1 Thess 5:17), isn't a legalistic burden but a sustaining joy. Prayer is one of the many ways we train ourselves for godliness. Someone once said that a regular habit of prayer will regulate everything else. At this point, Daniel was in his eighties, and we have every reason to assume that for nearly seven decades, regular prayer had had a significant hand in shaping him into such a strong man of God. It had deepened his relationship with God to the point that Daniel had no fear of the lions' den. Thus the irony: "Although it is Daniel's spiritual discipline of regular prayer that gives his enemies that opportunity to get him into trouble, that same discipline is his source of strength to stand firm in that trouble. Here's a lesson about the value of such spiritual discipline." Biblical prayer is more likely to change *us*, rather than our circumstances. In times of suffering and persecution, prayer becomes a sweet escape from harsh reality. It ushers us into God's throne room that we might become intoxicated with his majesty and be reminded that nothing on earth or in hell can sabotage his plan. Prayer can make even a den of lions seem as cozy as a Holiday Inn Express.

45. Rover Manvell and Heinrich Fraenkel, *The Men Who Tried to Kill Hitler* (New York: Skyhorse, 2008), 177.

# 7

# FOUR FOR FIGHTING

May I be irreverently honest for a moment?

When I finally decided my next book would be on Daniel, the choice came with significant reservation—there was no way I could avoid chapters 7–12 any longer. I ducked and dodged them for a while before actually reading them. When I did, my worst fears were confirmed. I'm not joking; these chapters intimidate me. While studying them, I would leave the office every day with a splitting headache. I lost track of how many times I wanted to plunge a screwdriver through my hand. They're weird and goofy. The stoic, levelheaded Daniel of chapters 1–6 seems to give way to a psychedelic Daniel on LSD in chapters 7–12.[1]

To make matters worse, everyone has an opinion on what these chapters mean, and some have very *strong* opinions. Are they a roadmap to the end of all things? You can find a lot of scholars and televangelists who think so. Or do they solely concern past events with no present relevance? I initially thought that attempting to teach or write on these chapters was as prudent as installing a microwave in your swimming pool. But after studying these chapters, I'm now in love with their grand vision

---

1. "Now that we have gotten used to the rather straightforward plots of Daniel 1–6 we suddenly find ourselves in a strange world, a world of hybrid beasts and riders on the clouds. Furthermore, we encounter what look like timetables, but timetables that are impossible to penetrate … What are we to make of these images and dreamlike numbers?" (Longman, *Daniel*, 177–78).

of the glory of God and his faithfulness to his people.

There are two main dangers concerning Dan 7–12. The first is to be so intimidated by them that you pretend they don't exist. I was tempted to do that. "People will be fine with a book on Daniel that only covers the first six chapters," I thought. Yet the second is to be so obsessed with making sense of every detail that you ignore the whole. Worse, you attempt to force the rest of Scripture through the grid of Dan 7–12, and that can be disastrous.[2] It's best to acknowledge these six chapters as a part of God's Word (not the sum of it), that they can offer us hope (Rom 15:4), make us wise for salvation in Christ, teach us about righteousness, and equip us for every good work (2 Tim 3:15–17).

Compared to the other visions in Daniel, this first one is the most alluded to in the NT,[3] but it also remains "one of the most enigmatic sections of the Old Testament."[4] That means this is a profoundly important chapter, but that the odds are against our understanding it correctly *and* completely. As is the case with the rest of Daniel, this chapter is not for the faint of heart, nor will it set well with those who desire nice and tidy answers to their biblical or theological questions.

What this chapter *will* do is give you an exalted view of God, cause you to bow in worship before the throne, to glory in being a member of his eternal kingdom, and to anticipate the return of Christ like a child waiting for Christmas morning. That's what all Scripture should do: compel worship, realign our priorities, and fill our hearts with joyful expectation. So maybe Dan 7–12 won't be as strange as we might think!

## APOCALYPTIC LITERATURE

A very small but important genre in Scripture is apocalyptic literature,

---

2. Baldwin, *Daniel*, 136.

3. "It would be no exaggeration to say that this chapter is one of the most important passages of the OT," (E. W. Heaton, *The Book of Daniel* [London: SCM Press, 1956], 169).

4. Longman, *Daniel*, 179.

one that was very familiar to Jews and Christians from about 200 B.C. to A.D. 200. But it's not as familiar to God's people in the 21st century.

> For most people apocalyptic literature represents one of the most fascinating and yet most mystifying portions of Scripture. When studying Daniel or Revelation, readers feel they have been transported into a fairy-tale world of myths and monsters, a Tolkien-type panorama of fantasy. The unreality of the symbols and the constant shifting from one mysterious scene to another is greatly confusing.[5]

What exactly is this literary genre? Simply put, "The apocalyptic teaching of the Bible gives us a vision of the future that generates hope in the present."[6] Apocalyptic comes from the Greek *apokalypto,* meaning "to reveal." This literature appears prominently in Daniel and Revelation, but also in parts of Isaiah, Ezekiel, and Zechariah, not to mention Jewish literature from the inter-testamental period (e.g. 1 Enoch).[7] Generally speaking, apocalyptic literature gives us earth-bound creatures a back-stage pass to events in the spiritual realm. It does so as a means of encouraging God's people suffering severe trials.[8]

A few important rules for reading and interpreting apocalyptic literature:

---

5. Grant R. Osborne, *The Hermeneutical Spiral,* 2nd ed. (Downers Grove, IL: InterVarsity Press, 2006), 275.

6. Tremper Longman III, *Reading the Bible with Heart and Mind* (Colorado Springs: NavPress, 1997), 226.

7. In all, D. S. Russell lists seventeen books that fit into the apocalyptic category (*The Method and Message of Jewish Apocalyptic* [Philadelphia: Westminster, 1964], 37–38).

8. "From the position of those who are safely removed from the action of tyrants and protected from the threat of martyrdom, we are not readily given to appreciate the situation of those for whom these words were written. Apocalyptic was born of catastrophe, and those to whom it was initially addressed were the potential victims of that catastrophe. For them the failure to understand the purposes of God, even when these were communicated in some way to them, must itself have been a nearly intolerable burden," (Anderson, *Signs and Wonders,* 99).

***Don't force literalness.*** "God both reveals and conceals as He speaks to us in the apocalyptic poetic images. He informs us accurately but not with precision. We get the basic point but not necessarily all the details."[9] The grossest abuses of apocalyptic literature have occurred when well-meaning Bible students with a high regard for God's Word forced a literal interpretation on the text. Very seldom does apocalyptic literature plainly mean what it says, since it is presented with cryptic symbols (cf. Num 12:6–8), especially numeric ones. Aren't we in for a surprise when we learn "seventy" doesn't mean the arithmetic number between 69 and 71!

***Don't be dogmatic.*** In commenting on apocalyptic literature in general, and the book of Revelation in particular, Fee and Stuart warn, "No one should approach the Revelation without a proper degree of humility!"[10] The same goes for the apocalyptic portions of Daniel. For anyone who compulsively wants all Scripture to make perfect sense (that would be me), Dan 7–12 will resemble a wild stallion that cannot possibly be broken, a giant jigsaw puzzle with missing pieces, or a Rubik's cube whose sides were never color-matched in the first place. As I studied and reflected on Daniel's final chapters, I often had to differentiate between what I could prove and what I only suspected. I had to remind myself that not even Daniel, one very renowned for his wisdom (Ezek 28:3), was able to make sense of these visions without heaven's help. The ambiguous language and vague symbolism may be meant "to keep the reader from giving the future fulfillment too great a place in the message of the book. The writer wanted to turn the reader toward God, not just toward future events."[11] False teachers such as Edgar Whisenant or Harold Camping dogmatically imposed a literal interpretation on the text, but they shipwrecked people's faith when their predictions failed to materialize. Let us be bold with what we can absolutely prove via a responsible handling

---

9. Longman, *Reading the Bible*, 219.

10. Gordon D. Fee and Douglas Stuart, *How to Read the Bible for All Its Worth*, 3rd ed. (Grand Rapids: Zondervan, 2003), 250.

11. Osborne, *The Hermeneutical Spiral*, 287.

of the text, but let us also be humble and admit "I don't know" when a sure interpretation eludes us.

***Don't miss the forest for the trees.*** In trying to decipher every symbol, don't get so bogged down that you miss the main message. As Paul encouraged Timothy after a few cryptic statements, "Consider what I say, for the Lord will give you understanding in everything" (2 Tim 2:7 HCSB). One does not have to have perfect understanding of Dan 7–12 to be comforted by its message. That God chose to communicate certain things through visions, rather than plain speech, may indicate his desire to arouse our emotions more than instruct the mind.[12] Just as it has done for God's people for more than 2,500 years, allow these visions from Daniel to inspire your faith in the eventual triumph of God's purposes.

## DANIEL 7:1–14

This vision dates to the first year of Belshazzar's reign (c. 550–549 B.C.),[13] meaning it took place sometime between Dan 4–5. Belshazzar was coregent with his father, Nabonidus, and Babylon was just a decade away from falling to the Medes and Persians. It was in 550 B.C. that Cyrus usurped the throne from Astyages the Mede and forged a new empire; though few realized it at the time, the political landscape of the known world was headed for violent change. This vision gave Daniel notice of what was still to come.

In a night dream, Daniel saw "the four winds of heaven were stirring up the great sea" (7:2). Elsewhere in the OT, "the great sea" refers exclusively to the Mediterranean (e.g. Num 34:6–7; Josh 1:4; Ezek 47:10; 48:28). But given the apocalyptic nature of this passage, this sea may be better identified as the cosmic sea present at the beginning (Gen 1:2),

---

12. "It's a dangerous thing to study prophecy just to satisfy our curiosity or to give people the impression that we are "great Bible students." If divine truth doesn't touch our own hearts and affect our conduct, then our Bible study is only an intellectual exercise to inflate our own ego," (Warren W. Wiersbe, *Be Resolute* [Colorado Springs: Victor, 2000], 93).

13. Gerhard F. Hasel, "The First and Third Years of Belshazzar," *AUSS* 15 (1977): 153–68.

and it thus "evokes horror and an anticipation of evil,"[14] (cf. Pss 89:9; 93:3–4; Isa 17:12; 57:20; Rev 13:1; 17:15; 21:1). But it is not outside the scope of God's control (Pss 18:15; 77:16; 93:3–4; 104:6–9; 107:23–29; 114:3; Nah 1:4). Consistent with the concept of God's "wind" or "Spirit" elsewhere in Scripture (e.g. Gen 1:2; John 3:8), the "four winds of heaven" are God's agent to exert his will on nations and peoples (cf. Jer 49:36; Zech 2:6; Rev 7:1).

From the sea, Daniel observed the emergence of four beasts[15] representing four empires. Even today, animals often symbolize various countries (e.g. Russian bear, Chinese dragon, American eagle) and U.S. states (Alaskan grizzly, Florida alligator, Texas longhorn). As you read about the four beasts, remember that they have no claim to the blessing of "very good" (Gen 1:31). They are mutants or hybrids (cf. "like a ...," 7:4–6), rather than animals that reproduced after their kind (Gen 1:25; cf. Deut 22:9–11). They are a perversion of what God created, a distortion of God's will, but they nonetheless remain under his sovereign control.

The first beast was a lion with wings, representing the Babylonian Empire and Nebuchadnezzar. Archaeologists have found numerous statues of winged lions in the ruins of Babylon.[16] Both the empire and Nebuchadnezzar are compared to a lion and eagle elsewhere in the OT (Jer 4:7–8; 48:40; 49:19, 22; 50:17, 44–46; Lam 4:19; Ezek 17:3, 12; Hab 1:8). That "the mind of a man" was given to this beast reminds the reader of the humiliation and restoration of Nebuchadnezzar (Dan 4:28–37; cf. Ps 49:20). The beast's feathers are plucked in the vision, marking "a loss of ferocity and power, which was most certainly the case in the last

14. "In the psyche of the people of the ancient Near East the sea was more than a dangerous place. It was a threatening force that was ranged against the beneficial forces of creation," (Longman, *Daniel*, 182).

15. "Composite beasts of the sort here encountered were regularly used in Babylonian art and examples may be seen in collections of art and in archaeological objects," (Jack P. Lewis, *The Major Prophets* [Henderson, TN: Hester Publications, 1999], 143).

16. Miller, *Daniel*, 197.

decades of the once all-conquering Babylonian regime."[17]

The next beast was a bear, second only to the lion in Scripture as a symbol of fierceness and power (cf. 1 Sam 17:34; 2 Sam 17:8; Prov 28:15; Isa 11:7; Lam 3:10; Hos 13:8; Amos 5:19) This beast is most often assumed to represent the Medo-Persian regime that conquered Babylon during Belshazzar's reign at the instigation of the Lord (Jer 51:11). The bear was depicted as raised up on one side, possibly an allusion to the unequal balance of Persia over Media (cf. 8:3). In the vision, the bear was gnawing on three bones; Cyrus conquered three kingdoms (Media, Anatolia, and Lydia) to forge his empire before moving on to additional conquests such as Babylon and Egypt ("eat your fill of flesh!" 7:5 NIV). But it's entirely plausible that three is meant to be symbolic, indicating "the insatiable nature of the beast,"[18] i.e. its greedy appetite for additional conquest.[19]

The third beast, a leopard- or panther-like creature known for its swiftness (Jer 5:6; Hos 13:7; Hab 1:8), had four wings and heads. It likely symbolized Alexander the Great's rule that spread across the earth like wildfire (cf. 2:39), only to be divided between his four generals (cf. 8:8, 22) following Alexander's death in Nebuchadnezzar's old palace in Babylon (ironic, no?). "Dominion" or "authority" (NIV) was given to this beast, meaning Alexander's reign was divinely appointed and did not come by his own ability.

As fearsome as each was in its own right, the three beasts did not compare to the fourth, the one that scared Daniel most. He piled on the adjectives, describing it as "terrifying and dreadful and exceedingly strong." "This beast has no counterpart in the realm of nature."[20] Daniel

17. Anderson, *Signs and Wonders*, 79.

18. Young, *Daniel*, 145. "The greedy expansionism of nations can evidently have a place within the purpose of God," (Goldingay, *Daniel*, 186).

19. "The brown Syrian bear may weigh up to 250 kilos [550 pounds] and has a voracious appetite," (Baldwin, *Daniel*, 139).

20. Hailey, *Daniel*, 135.

particularly noticed the beast's iron teeth and ten horns,[21] the latter not a literal number, but a symbolic one meaning a large number of kings. An eleventh horn, a small one, rose up and displaced three of the previous ten. It had a man's eyes and spoke "great things" (i.e. it "spoke arrogantly," HCSB), which did not bode well for the little horn or the beast (cf. Ps 12:3–4; Obad 12, Rev 13:5–6). That it had eyes and a mouth make it almost certain that this little horn represented a man, not an entire kingdom.

At this point, Daniel's vision shifted away from the sea to the throne room of God, the Ancient of Days (cf. Pss 90:2; 93:2; Jer 23:18, 22). The aura is suddenly different from before. Where there had formerly been chaos, hostility, and oppression, there is now goodness and justice and order. It is God's prerogative to judge the entire world, and he does so with justice (Pss 9:7–8; 98:9). The Ancient of Days is described as having white clothes and hair, a symbol of his holiness and purity (Ps 51:7; Isa 1:18; Matt 17:2), and as enthroned upon wheels[22] and aflame with fire, marking his omniscience and righteous judgment (Pss 50:3; 97:3; Ezek 1:26–29). Enthroned in incomparable majesty, the Lord was surrounded by a vast multitude of angels (cf. 1 Kgs 22:19; Ps 82:1; Rev 5:11–14; 7:11).

In the ANE, a daily record was kept of events in the kingdom (cf. Ezra 4:15; Esth 6:1). John's vision in Rev 20 mentions two books to be opened on Judgment Day: the books that contain a record of all the deeds of the earth (Ps 56:8; Mal 3:16), and the book of life in which the names of the righteous are recorded (12:1; Exod 32:32; Ps 69:28; Luke 10:20). It seems the former book is the one referenced in Dan 7. When "the books were opened," the wickedness of the fourth beast was recounted. Daniel then witnessed the fourth beast being killed, destroyed, and consumed with fire (cf. Isa 9:5; 66:24 Rev 19:20; 20:10), presumably the same fire emanating like volcanic lava from God's throne. I'd say only a greasy spot remained where the fourth beast had been, but given the totality of God's judgment

21. In the OT, a horn is a symbol of power (Deut 33:17; 1 Sam 2:1, 10; Ps 18:2; Zech 1:18, 21).

22. It was common for thrones in ancient times to have wheels (Lacocque, *Daniel*, 143).

and wrath against this beast, I doubt even a greasy spot remained! The three other beasts were stripped of their power, but their lives were prolonged.

Then Daniel witnessed One "like a son of man" (i.e. One who looked like a man, rather than a beast) coming "with the clouds of heaven" (not emerging from the sea) and stood before God. To this "man" was given dominion, glory, and a kingdom (cf. Ps 2:8)—none of which would ever pass away (in contrast to the beasts and their finite dominion). This figure cannot be any other than Christ, the person of God who became a man.[23] "Son of Man" was his most common self-description, occurring over eighty times in the Gospels. In OT poetry, God is often said to ride the clouds like a chariot (Pss 68:4; 104:3; Isa 19:1; Jer 4:13), and Jesus spoke of his doing the same (Matt 24:30; Mark 13:26),[24] particularly on the eve of his crucifixion (Matt 26:64; Mark 14:62).

## DANIEL 7:15–27

Daniel was deeply troubled by this vision and asked one of the angels standing at the throne for an explanation. The four beasts represented four earthly kingdoms, and God's people would possess the eternal kingdom given to the son of man (cf. Matt 5:3; 10). But Daniel could not shake the frightening threat of the fourth beast, one "different from all the rest" (7:19), as well as the ten horns and the little horn. Specifically, Daniel had witnessed the little horn persecute and prevail over God's people, but only until the Ancient of Days passed judgment.

Lest Daniel be unduly concerned about this fourth beast, he was emphatically assured that the heavenly court would convene, the Almighty would strip the little horn of its power, and the beast as a whole would be utterly destroyed by God's judgment. Moreover, an eternal kingdom

23. Some scholars consider this son-of-man figure to be the archangel Michael, but while the book of Daniel gives Michael a prominent role in the spiritual realm, "it hardly pictures him as the eternal king of the world," (Chisholm, *Handbook on the Prophets*, 309).

24. "Among the Jews the Messiah came to be known as 'anani 'Cloudy One' or bar nivli 'Son of the Cloud,'" (Young, *Daniel*, 154).

would be established, and God's people would inherit it forever. Only then was Daniel told more about the deeds of the little horn. Despite this comfort, however, the dream continued to haunt Daniel. What are we to make of this strange vision?

As was the case in Dan 2, this chapter alludes to four different empires, but there is no consensus as to how they should be identified. In fact, obtaining a scholarly consensus on most anything in Dan 7–12 is as likely as getting a bus full of adolescents to agree on where to eat lunch on a long road trip. The majority of conservative scholars consider the four empires to be Babylon, Media-Persia, Greece, and Rome; this is certainly the oldest and most popular interpretation. Liberal scholars say the four empires are Babylon, Media, Persia, and Greece, though Media and Persia are never considered two separate empires in Daniel (cf. 5:28; 6:8, 12, 15; 8:20).

I consider the fourth empire to be Rome. Daniel told Nebuchadnezzar that the kingdom of heaven would be established "in the days of" the fourth empire (2:44); in the NT, both John the Baptist and Jesus preached that the kingdom of heaven was near (Matt 3:2; 4:17) while Rome ruled supreme. After Jesus' resurrection and ascension, it is said that Christians had been ushered into the kingdom (Col 1:13), that they had received an unshakable kingdom (Heb 12:28). In other words, all signs point to the fulfillment of 2:44; 7:14 as occurring in the person and work of Jesus. But I have a few reservations with identifying the fourth empire as Rome:

1. Of the four empires in Dan 2, 7, the only one explicitly identified for us is the first, Babylon. Interpreters subjectively identify the rest with various shades of certainty. I'm not sure "four" isn't meant to be symbolic of something else.[25] "To seek to identify these kingdoms,

25. Coffman points out, "'Four' in the numerology of the Hebrews is the number of the earth; and what is indicated here is that monstrous world-governments shall continue throughout the world's history," (*Daniel*, 119). "Daniel in this vision saw these beasts and horns not simply as each having its own historical identity, but also as each being a typical example of the kind of empire and the kind of petty satellite power that can and will arise, here and there, now and then, in the field of human history under various different circumstances as time moves

when Scripture furnishes no clue as to their identity, is very precarious and probably unwarranted."[26]

2. How was Rome vastly different from the previous three empires (7:7)? Was it in its power, longevity, or influence? Rome certainly wasn't superior in terms of territorial size—Alexander's empire was larger. And how can we explain historically the fourth beast being destroyed, while the other three were prolonged for a time (7:12)?[27]
3. Whether the coming of the son of man in the clouds alludes to Jesus' ascension or the Second Coming, in what way was the Roman Empire destroyed right before these two events?

The ten horns are considered parallel to the ten toes of the statue in Dan 2, but the text never explicitly says how many toes the statue had. For those who consider the fourth empire to be Rome, the ten toes/horns are said to be ten emperors, yet no one can agree on which ten. Do we start with Caesar Augustus, making Domitian the little horn?[28] Or Pompey, with Vespasian as the little horn?[29] If you identify the fourth empire with Greece, the ten horns/toes are said to be ten Greek kings culminating with Antiochus IV as the little horn, though this Antiochus was eighth in the dynasty, not eleventh.[30] Still others identify the ten horns with a

on to the fulfillment of God's great purposes with mankind," (Wallace, *The Lord Is King,* 131).

26. Young, *Daniel,* 149–50.

27. It's often suggested that Babylon, Persia, and Greece lived on as provinces or territories, but how is this different historically from Rome's fate after its collapse?

28. McGuiggan, *Daniel,* 130–33. Domitian fits the profile of the little horn as much as anyone else, but no one can sufficiently explain how he "put down three kings" (7:24).

29. Turner, *Daniel,* 109–19. Vespasian was certainly an enemy of Judaism since Jerusalem was destroyed under his authority in A.D. 70, but this event only affected those Jews who had rejected Christ, which one could hardly consider to be the "saints" of 7:25. Additionally, Vespasian never elevated himself to divine status (McGuiggan, *Daniel,* 135).

30. If the fourth kingdom in Dan 2, 7 is Greece, and the little horn is Antiochus, how was

post-Rome or revived-Rome reality like the European Common Market (today's European Union),[31] and the little horn with Mohammed, Napoleon, one of the popes (or the papacy as a whole), or with Paul's man of lawlessness (2 Thess 2:1–12), i.e. a future Antichrist figure. I have my own nominees for the identity of the little horn, including Jerry Jones, Microsoft, and whoever invented reality television.

And what of the "time, times, and half a time" (7:25)? Is it to be interpreted literally as 3½? If so, are we dealing with 3½ *years* or centuries?[32] The phrase "is in itself a chronologically indefinite expression."[33] Just as seven "times" in Dan 4 did not necessarily mean seven years, this phrase in Dan 7 is likely meant to stand for a broken seven, the biblical number of perfection. This phrase, along with 42 months (i.e. 3½ years), refers to a period of intense persecution of God's people in John's Apocalypse (cf. Rev 11:2–3; 12:6, 14; 13:4–5).

I'm rather confused at this point, so it might help to revisit the three principles for interpreting apocalyptic literature. Expecting the four empires, the ten horns, or the three uprooted horns[34] to be literal may not be warranted.[35] Nailing down the identity of the little horn has also proven slippery. We certainly have no reason to be dogmatic about our interpretations of a chapter so fraught with disagreement, but nor should

---

the kingdom of God established with his demise?

31. There was a lot of breathless anticipation of the Second Coming when the European Common Market became ten nations. When it added its eleventh and twelfth members, the giddiness subsided. Today, the European Union has 28 members.

32. Most interpreters see the phrase as meaning 3½ years (cf. 12:7, 11–12). Turner believed it alluded to the 3½ centuries that Rome persecuted the church (*Daniel*, 134–39).

33. Young, *Daniel*, 161.

34. Hailey believes the three horns usurped by the little horn are not three definite rulers, but "a symbolic number representing those whom God suffered to be taken out of the way" by the little horn (*Daniel*, 144).

35. Ferguson likens this to finding hidden meaning in the minute details of Jesus' parables. "This is to fail to grasp the genre of the passage whose details do not have one-to-one equivalents," (*Daniel*, 162).

we miss the forest for the trees. So what is this chapter really saying?

The general picture presented to Daniel is that God has established human government (Rom 13:1), but that they often have a beastly side in that they do not always honor him as God (Rom 1:21–23).[36] Instead, as we saw in Dan 3–6, elements in government can blasphemously elevate themselves to the level of God. But as dismal a picture as we have in 7:25, it is followed by the promise of 7:26, that God's righteous judgment and fierce fury are the destiny of every tyrant. Just when it seems God's people are being persecuted without restraint, the period of oppression is cut short. To be sure, the power of Satan lies behind all spiritual powers and tyrants that "wear out the saints of the Most High." But God never relinquishes control. He only allows his people to be oppressed for a time, and never the whole allotted time. Just as "time, times, and half a time" is a broken seven, so I believe God breaks in half any season of trial for his people as an act of mercy (cf. Matt 24:22). The throne room scene in Dan 7 reminds us that God will one day judge the world through Jesus (Acts 17:31). Just as Satan and the beast are to be cast into the fire (Rev 20:10), so will every arrogant empire and emperor that ignores God (Isa 13:11). But those whose faith and hope are in Jesus, the Son of Man, will be vindicated.

> See the picture. The saints walk into the judgment room beaten and battered but still claiming that the kingdom is theirs. The beast comes snorting and roaring into the courtroom claiming the kingdom is his. God renders a verdict in favor of the saints, the beast is judged and the kingdom is given to the saints.[37]

This is a kingdom not limited to Jews, but for "all peoples, nations,

---

36. Daniel "lived and operated much closer to the realities of earthly government than falls to the lot of most of us, and was therefore fully aware of the dimension of terror inherent in the placing of power in the hands of sinful men," (Wallace, *The Lord Is King*, 135).

37. McGuiggan, *Daniel*, 144.

and languages" (7:14; cf. Gal 3:26–29; Rev 7:9). These are the true holy ones—the saints—of God.

Every September, two of my great loves come into violent conflict: ministry and Dallas Cowboys football. From time to time, their schedule conflicts with my commitment to worship with the saints and other church activities, so I simply record the game on my DVR and watch it later. The only problem is that I don't have the self-discipline *not* to check the score beforehand; most times, I already know the final outcome when I sit down to watch the recorded game. If I know Dallas won, I don't panic over a turnover, missed field goal, or blown call like I would while watching it live (I take my football seriously). Knowing the final outcome gives me peace in troubled times. It is therefore significant that Daniel was not shown the full extent of the little horn's horror until *after* he had witnessed the victory of the Son of Man.[38] Nothing in this chapter gives us a detailed roadmap for what lies ahead, but the symbolism works to inform us of the final outcome: God wins and Jesus reigns.

That should give us peace in troubled times.

THROUGHOUT THE 19th century, many people believed the human condition was substantially improving at a rapid pace. This notion was seemingly validated as the Industrial Revolution gained steam and the standard of living increased in developed countries. It climaxed with the end of World War I, one that was billed as "the war to end all wars." And then, scarcely two decades later, World War II came along. Then the Iron Curtain, the Cold War and its Cuban Missile crisis, and the Vietnam conflict. No sooner had the Berlin Wall fallen than global terrorism became the new threat. Even now, with the advances of space exploration and the digital age, we're still dealing with sin and corruption on an international scale.

38. Wallace, *The Lord Is King*, 136.

Remember how I mentioned Nebuchadnezzar's statue in Dan 2 was comprised of precious metals of declining worth, but also increasing hardness or "severity"? Did you notice that, of the four beasts, the last was more ferocious than the others? Such is a reminder that the human experience is getting worse, not better. Since Eden, human history has been on a spiraling descent *away from* Utopia. The world is now worse off overall than it was in Daniel's day, and the one our great-grandchildren will inherit will be inferior to our own.

This realization proves this world holds nothing for us, whereas heaven holds all. This does not mean we should eschew Jeremiah's advice to the Judean captives, to seek the good of our cities and pray for their prosperity, but the prophet also reminded the captives that they would one day return home (Jer 29:7, 10). Likewise, as citizens of heaven, Christians living on earth must constantly remind themselves of the priories and values of their homeland. In spite of the terrible realities of war, recession, poverty, and social injustice, the people of God have no reason to fear the troubled future.

One day, God will send his Son from heaven to usher in the new heavens and earth "where righteousness dwells" (2 Pet 3:13 NIV). Persecution is our lot on earth (2 Tim 3:12), but evil and suffering are unwelcome in that land fairer than day (Matt 5:4; Rev 21:4). Like Daniel, present circumstances and future threats might alarm us, but our hope is in the Son of Man coming in the clouds (Mark 13:26–27; John 14:1–3; 1 Thess 4:13–18). On that day, the saints of God will be vindicated, and everlasting joy in God's presence will become our reward. On that day, we will see the knee of every tyrant kneel before the Son of Man (Phil 2:10). On that day, God will be glorified (Phil 2:11).

What a day, glorious day, that will be.

## TALKING POINTS

There exists in your heart and mine a beast capable of unmitigated atrocities. Democrats think the beast lives in corporations, and Republicans believe it to be in government, but the Bible says the beast is in all of us. One of most difficult things for us to do is come to grips with our terrible sinfulness. We call our sins "mistakes" as if we left the house wearing mismatched shoes. But both the disturbing imagery of Dan 7 and our own experiences confront us with the fact that "the beast is in the heart of each one of us."[39] In no uncertain terms, Paul declared both Jews and Gentiles guilty of moral atrocities (Rom 1:18-3:20). "None is righteous, no, not one; no one understands; no one seeks for God" (Rom 3:10–11). But the apostle later imagined another courtroom scene in Rom 8. "Who shall bring any charge against God's elect? ... Who is to condemn?" (Rom 8:33–34). Paul makes clear in this glorious passage that we have no reason to fear God's judgment if we are in Christ. Citizens of the kingdom are no longer under condemnation (Rom 8:1). A righteous verdict has been guaranteed for us! Against any angel, ruler, evil power, "we are more than conquerors through him who loved us" (Rom 8:37)! Though the beast is in each of us, God in Christ proved to us the depths of his love. Let this truth inspire you and guide you as you go through life. Like Stephen, I pray in your final hours that you're given a vision of the Son of Man enthroned in incomparable majesty (Acts 7:56). With your dying breath, may you be reminded of your great sin and your even greater Savior. And may the moment after that find you kneeling in worship before that Savior with these words on your lips: "To him who sits on the throne and to the Lamb be blessing and honor and glory and might forever and ever!" (Rev 5:13).

I have a filter on my web browser that weeds out all political status updates on Facebook and replaces them with old presidential

39. Longman, *Daniel*, 195.

campaign ads. I found this filter particularly useful during the 2012 presidential election. I'm rather conservative in my politics, but the faithful of both parties became juvenile and annoying. So it was nice to see an ad encouraging me to vote for William Henry Harrison or Harry Truman, instead of a regurgitated sound byte. I also wish I had another filter, one through which I could run every tweet and status update, a filter based on 7:14. "To him [Christ] was given dominion and glory and a kingdom, that all peoples, nations, and languages should serve him; his dominion is an everlasting dominion, which shall not pass away, and his kingdom one that shall not be destroyed." You and I would be better off if we spent less time worrying about gun control, runaway deficit spending, and where/how long the president spends his vacation. We would be better served worrying less about how Liberals, Conservatives, Muslims, Atheists, or others not like us are destroying America. Instead, how would things be different if we confessed daily that Jesus, even now, held dominion over all the earth (Matt 28:18)? What would it look like if we spent more time urging people to willingly kneel before King Jesus now before being compelled to do so on the final day (Phil 2:10–11)? What would it look like if more Christians spent less time griping about earthly empires destined for history's trash heap, and celebrated instead Jesus' indestructible and eternal kingdom? How would our words on social media and in the real world be different if our refuge was in Christ (Ps 2:12), rather than our favorite politician or party? Can someone program for me a Facebook filter like that?

# 8

# GOT YOUR GOAT

Among my favorite movies is *Bruce Almighty,* the story of a news reporter suddenly given power by the Almighty to exercise divine prerogative and right a few wrongs. Along with the miraculous ability to part his tomato soup as if it were the Red Sea and transform his clunker car into a sporty Saleen S7, Bruce also had to answer prayers. The prayers became so voluminous that he eventually began affirming all the requests. God's (i.e. Morgan Freeman's) response to such a strategy is a stinging indictment of human nature: "Since when do people have a clue what they want?"

It requires faith to see things from God's perspective, but when we do, we quickly realize how the wrong things attract us and the right things seem abominable. We blame God in poor situations, but we credit karma or count our lucky stars when things look up. How could we have a clue about what we really want—much less need?

One of the reasons Dan 8 is such a remarkable chapter is that it contains a very detailed, predictive prophecy concerning the fate of the Jews 400 years after Daniel. Take a moment and let that significance sink in. It is no less startling than someone uttering a prophecy in 16th-century Europe that proved to be a play-by-play of World War II or the Cold War. Such a prophecy would be considered more remarkable since major players in these wars (most notably the U.S.) weren't yet settled nations in the 16th century.

This, then, is how the validity of Scripture is verified. Coffman says, "This chapter stands as the irrefutable example of genuine predictive prophecy at its most excellent achievement."[1] As we will see, the predictions made in this chapter most certainly came to pass just as God promised, arguably down to the very day. Ironically, the predictions of Dan 8 are so accurate that some scholars allege the prophecies of the chapter were made *ex eventu* (i.e. after the fact). Yet these are only the objections of those prejudiced against the miraculous.

That said, the effect of this prophecy was not so much to give the Jews a detailed itinerary of the future, but to encourage them to maintain trust in the God of heaven. The vision initially unsettled Daniel significantly, but I think he eventually saw it as proof that God would be with Israel, even in the darkest of times. If the Lord knew the future so intimately and exactly, "declaring the end from the beginning" (Isa 46:10), then surely he could be trusted to work events to Israel's good and his glory. Left to ourselves, we wouldn't want to endure years of harsh persecution, but since when do people have a clue what they want? If God could use Paul's imprisonment to further the gospel (Phil 1:12–14); if God could use the worst day in history, a day now known as "Good Friday," to bless his people, then nothing is out of his control. This chapter gives us the assurance that God knows the future, that he is Lord of all, and that it is up to us to trust him in all things, for thereby we overcome the world (1 John 5:4).

## DANIEL 8:1–14

This vision took place in Belshazzar's third year (548–547 B.C.).[2] God's Spirit[3] took Daniel to Susa, particularly to the Ulai canal, a body

1. Coffman, *Daniel*, 127.

2. Hasel, "First and Third Years," 153–68.

3. Though the text does not say so explicitly, this is the belief of most every scholar considering the parallels to Ezek 3:12; 8:2–3; 11:1; 40:1; Rev 17:3. It is further argued that Daniel could not have been in Susa since, just a few days after the vision, he resumed his job 200

of water on Susa's NE side. Susa was a fortress-city about 200 miles east of Babylon. At the time of this vision, it was the capital of Elam. Later, Susa served as the winter residence for Persian kings until Darius I made it his capital in 521 and built a palace there (cf. Neh 1:1; Esth 1:2). Later, Josephus called Susa "the metropolis of Persia" (*Antiquities* 10.269).[4]

Unlike the previous chapter, which was a dream, this was a vision during which Daniel was awake and conscious. In the vision, he saw on the canal's bank a ram with one horn higher than the other (a very unusual detail). It charged to the west, north, and south and proved invincible. "He did as he pleased and became great" (8:4). Then a male goat appeared, charging furiously from the west with such speed that it didn't touch the ground. For the OT prophets, horns most always symbolized power and military might, while rams and male goats represented oppressive leadership (Jer 51:40; Ezek 34:17; 39:18; Zech 10:3).

Daniel observed this goat's "conspicuous" horn. "In his powerful wrath," the goat charged at the ram with rage and broke the ram's two horns, then trampled and vanquished him (note that the goat's wrath stood out to Daniel). The goat, in turn, "became exceedingly great" (8:8), meaning it was presumptuous or arrogant.[5] But then its horn was broken and four more "conspicuous horns" rose up in its place "toward the four winds of heaven."

That's when "a little horn" also rose up and became "exceedingly great," particularly toward the south, east, and "the glorious land," i.e. Palestine (Ps 106:24; Jer 3:19; Ezek 20:6, 15; Zech 7:14), God's inheritance to his people and the place the captives longed to return (Ps 137:1–6). The rise of the little horn reached "the host of heaven," and it trampled some of the

---

miles away in Babylon. Contra Josephus (*Antiquities* 10.11.7) and Archer ("Daniel," 101), who believe Daniel was physically present at the Ulai canal. Turner concurs, arguing that Nabonidus had demoted Daniel and stationed him in Susa, rather than in Babylon (*Daniel*, 146–47).

4. "Its very geographical setting made clear that it [this vision] did not relate to the period of the exile but to later circumstances," (Goldingay, *Daniel*, 219).

5. Young, *Daniel*, 169.

host and stars of heaven, likely meaning the people of Israel (cf. Gen 15:5; 22:17; Exod 7:4; 12:41).[6] The little horn became "as great as the Prince of the host" to the point that the regular burnt offering was stripped away and the sanctuary overthrown. Some of the host and the Temple services would be given to it; the little horn would "throw truth to the ground, and it will act and prosper."

At that point in the vision, two holy ones (i.e. angels, cf. 4:13, 23) began conversing. One asked the other how long these things would last, a standard question posed to God in the OT concerning the suffering of his people (Pss 6:3; 80:4; 90:13; Isa 6:11; Hab 2:6; Zech 1:12; cf. Rev 6:10). I absolutely love this because it meant God's people would not be oppressed by this little horn forever. There is always an end to suffering, and it always comes in God's good timing. How long would the little horn be allowed to oppress God's people? The reply given to Daniel was "2,300 evenings and mornings," at which point the sanctuary would be restored. What are we to make of such a phrase, and of a little horn licensed with so much power?

## DANIEL 8:15–27

Having witnessed the vision, Daniel then saw a man (i.e. God; cf. Ezek 1:26, 28) "between the banks of the Ulai," meaning he was hovering over the water. The "man" commanded Gabriel[7] to explain the vision. That the vision was "for the time of the end" meant it concerned things that would happen at the end of a period of time, not the end of the world. Later, Gabriel said the vision concerned "the latter end of the indignation ... the appointed time of the end" (8:19), meaning God had appointed

6. "Stars" as a symbol of God's people can also be seen in 12:3; Phil 2:15; Rev 1:20. Jude 13 refers to false teachers as "wandering stars."

7. Gabriel is the first angel mentioned in Scripture; Michael is the only other. Jewish literature claimed there were a total of seven archangels: Suruel, Raphael, Raguel, Michael, Saraqael, Gabriel, and Remiel (1 Enoch 20:1–7). It appears Happy, Sneezy, Sleepy, Dopey, Grumpy, Bashful, and Doc were already taken.

a period of time in which he would punish his people for their sins[8] (cf. 2 Macc 6:12–17; 7:18), but he had also ordained an end for this terrible string of events. In other words, "the end" of 8:17 points back to the question of 8:13—"For how long?"[9] This vision is *not* about the end of the world; I can't stress enough how important this distinction is.[10]

The ram signified the Medo-Persian Empire.[11] The lesser horn was Media, a nation that was initially great, but conquered by the Persians in 550 B.C., at which point Cyrus fused the two kingdoms together—"the higher [horn] came up last" (8:3). From that point, Persia conquered nations to the west (Babylon, Syria, Lydia), north (Armenia, Scythia), and south (Egypt and Ethiopia). The Persian kingdom lasted more than 200 years and indeed "became great"—it amassed more territory than any other empire before it.

The goat was the Greek Empire,[12] and the first great horn was "the first king," known to us as Alexander the Great (1 Macc 1:1).[13] Born in

8. Baldwin says "the indignation" (8:19) is "the sentence of God which must eventually fall on those who rebel against him and fail to repent," even on God's chosen people (*Daniel*, 159).

9. Baldwin draws an excellent analogy between this passage's use of "the end" and Amos 8:2, wherein "the end" for Israel was not the end of time, but Assyrian captivity (cf. Ezek 21:25, 29; 35:5). Comparing Daniel and Amos, she concludes, "In each case the end meant the end of rebellion against God, because he intervened in judgment," (Ibid.; cf. Collins, *Daniel*, 338).

10. Drawing from the 2,300 days of Dan 8, a New York Baptist preacher named William Miller began advocating in 1831 that the return of Christ would occur in 1844—2,300 years from the decree of Artaxerxes in 457. The date was later narrowed to Oct 22, 1844. When that day came and went, it became known as the "Great Disappointment." Various leaders of the Restoration Movement were among Miller's followers. Today, a remnant lives on in the Seventh-day Adventists.

11. Persian kings sported a golden ram's head on their helmets whenever they led their armies into battle (Ammianus Marcellinus 19.1).

12. Albert Barnes gives evidence that the goat was a common symbol for Macedonia in ancient times (*Notes on the Old Testament: Daniel*, vol. 2 [Grand Rapids: Baker, 1950], 103–5).

13. Josephus relates a story, considered dubious by some as to its veracity, of how Alexander came to Jerusalem and was shown by the high priest this very passage in Daniel. "Wherein Daniel declared that one of the Greeks should destroy the empire of the Persians, he [Alexander] supposed that himself was the person intended." After reading the passage,

356, Alexander assumed his father's throne at age 20 when Philip II was assassinated. The goat's wrath and rage had caught Daniel's attention, and for good reason. "Enraged" (8:7) means "to be embittered" or "maddened."[14] Persia tried unsuccessfully to conquer Greece, but only succeeded in angering them. The campaigns of Darius I in 490 and of Xerxes a decade later had especially left many Greeks outraged, and Alexander exploited the memory of those events to inflame his troops. Within three short years, his army devastated Persian forces at the decisive battles of Granicus, Issus, and Arbela. Alexander "became exceedingly great" by conquering more territory than Persia had done (1 Macc 1:3), a total of some 1.5 million square miles stretching from Greece to India. Near the end of his life, he asked his troops and subjects to treat him as divine.[15] Alexander died eight years after conquering Persia—while returning to Babylon from India, he contracted what is believed to have been malaria. He crossed over the Styx on June 13, 323 B.C. at the young age of 32.

Just as Gabriel said, four separate kingdoms arose from Alexander's empire, but they did not have his power. None of them ever rivaled the glory and dominion he had forged in such a short amount of time; recall that the goat charged across the earth with such speed that it never touched the ground. When Alexander died, his kingdom was eventually divided among four of his generals, often known as the "Diadochi" (Greek for "successors"). Greece went to Cassander, Asia Minor to Lysimachus, Syria to Seleucus, and Egypt to Ptolemy.

Toward the end of the Greek Empire, one particular king (the little horn) with a "bold face" and the ability to understand "riddles" ascended the throne. As early as Josephus (*Antiquities* 10.276), there is virtually absolute consensus that this was the Seleucid king Antiochus IV.

Consider that:

---

Alexander then granted the Jews a few perks (*Antiquities* 11.8.5).

14. Young, *Daniel*, 169.

15. Miller, *Daniel*, 224.

This king, the little horn, would come to power "at the latter end of the indignation" and "when the transgressors have reached their limit" (8:19, 23). "Indignation" here means God's wrath against his unfaithful people (cf. 11:36; Isa 10:5; Lam 2:6). In the final OT book of Malachi (c. 450 B.C.), some of the Jews had again forsaken the Law. In the years leading up to Antiochus' reign, apostates had introduced the more pagan aspects of Greek culture into the practice of Judaism:

> They built a gymnasium in Jerusalem, according to Gentile custom, and removed the marks of circumcision, and abandoned the holy covenant. They joined with the Gentiles and sold themselves to do evil ... All the Gentiles accepted the command of the king. Many even from Israel gladly adopted his religion; they sacrificed to idols and profaned the Sabbath.
>
> 1 Macc 1:14–15, 43 NRSV

In short, "apostasy within Israel brought down a scourge upon Israel."[16]

This king would have a "bold face" (cf. "insolent" NASU), meaning he would be hard, determined, and unyielding (cf. Deut 28:50; Prov 7:13). He would be "one who understands riddles," i.e. he was politically savvy and skilled at flattery—cf. "a master trickster" (Msg), "skilled in double-dealing."[17] "The king is characterized by the claim and appearance of wisdom that is traditionally associated with Near Eastern kings, but ultimately that wisdom is shown to be perverse."[18] This fits the general portrait of Antiochus as presented by historians.

This king would have tremendous power, "but not by his own

16. Charles H. H. Wright, *Daniel and His Prophecies* (London: Williams, 1906), 181. Antiochus' "tyrannical rule over God's people is divine retribution for Israel's (unspecified) sin," (Hill, "Daniel," 150).

17. A. A. Bevan, *A Short Commentary on the Book of Daniel* (Cambridge: Univ. Press, 1892), 139.

18. Collins, *Daniel*, 340.

power." In other words, his power would not be earned, but be given to him by a superior. Antiochus gained his authority through less-than-noble means. His brother, Seleucus IV, was assassinated, and Antiochus assumed the throne only after incarcerating Seleucus' son Demetrius in Rome. During his reign, Antiochus enjoyed successful military exploits against Egypt ("toward the south," 8:9), Babylon, Persia ("toward the east"), and Palestine ("toward the glorious land").

This king would "cause fearful destruction." He would be successful in destroying "mighty men" and "the saints," and in making "deceit prosper" while he reigned. On one occasion, Antiochus launched a surprise attack against Jerusalem after assuring them he wanted peace (1 Macc 1:29–30). On another, he had several Jews attacked and massacred on the Sabbath, knowing they would not defend themselves on a day of rest (1 Macc 2:32–38).

This king would destroy a lot of people "without warning," and would even elevate himself against "the Prince of princes," i.e. God (cf. Isa 14:13). "In his own mind he shall become great" (8:25), which is a very key phrase. Antiochus assumed the title *Theou Epiphanes,* meaning "God manifest" or "God revealed," but his detractors amended it to *Epimanes,* meaning "madman." Antiochus "threw truth to the ground" by ordering Torah scrolls to be burned (1 Macc 1:56–57). The first king mentioned in the book of Daniel, Jehoiakim, discovered that bad things happen to those who toss aside the truth of God's Word (Jer 36:20–31); Antiochus would fare no better.

The inquiring angel particularly mentioned "the transgression that makes desolate" (8:13). In his vendetta against the God of heaven, Antiochus raided the Temple of its valuables and suspended the entire system of Temple worship to Yahweh, including the abolishment of the daily sacrifice[19] and suspension of religious feasts and practices (e.g. Passover, circumcision). Worse, he profaned the holy altar and desecrated

19. Baldwin echoes other scholars when she says the phrase "the regular burnt offering" (8:11) implies the whole sacrificial system (*Daniel,* 157).

the Temple in 167 by sacrificing a pig (1 Macc 1:20–23, 47, 54; 2 Macc 6:2–5). As Lucas explains, the phrase "abomination of desolation" is a derogatory pun on the name "Baal Shamen," the Aramaic form of "Zeus Olympios," the god to whom Antiochus sacrificed the swine (2 Macc 6:2).[20] To get an idea of just how blasphemous and offensive this was to the faithful in Israel, Russell likens it to a wave of vandalism in London about thirty years ago in which Jews found the tombstones of their deceased marred by swastikas. "What they saw was an obscenity, a spitting in the face of God."[21]

But then the king, the little horn, would be broken, "but by no human hand." Just as God had (via Satan) given Antiochus his power "for a purpose beyond his own knowing,"[22] God took his power away. Josephus relates how Antiochus besieged the Persian city of Elymais, but was rebuffed and had to flee to Babylon with a decimated army. At Babylon, he heard of how his forces in Judea had been defeated by the Maccabees. With his world crashing down around him, Antiochus "fell into a distemper." While on his deathbed, he confessed to his friends "that this calamity was sent upon him for the miseries he had brought upon the Jewish nation, while he plundered their temple and condemned their God," (*Antiquities* 12.9.1; cf. 1 Macc 6:1–16). Other ancient historians confirm Antiochus' death "by no human hand."[23]

Behold, the derision of heaven.

THIS TERRIBLE PERIOD of persecution was to last for 2,300 evenings and mornings, but what does this mean? To begin with,

20. Lucas, *Daniel*, 218.

21. Russell, *Daniel*, 148.

22. Anderson, *Signs and Wonders*, 102; cf. Miller, *Daniel*, 234.

23. Polybius records how Antiochus was "driven mad, as some say, by some manifestations of divine wrath," (*Histories* 31:11).

interpreters are divided over exactly what is meant.[24] Are we to read this as 2,300 days?[25] Or is it referring to 2,300 sacrifices, two a day (Exod 29:38–39; Num 28:3–8), meaning 1,150 days?[26] There is no consensus in sight. To compound the matter even further (as if it needed it), should we even interpret the number literally, rather than symbolically?

Those who interpret the 2,300 as 2,300 days point out that evening and morning constitute one full day in Gen 1. Since 2,300 equates to about 6½ years, it possibly alludes to the period between the murder of the high priest Onias III by his rival Menelaus in 170 B.C. and the rededication of the Temple by Judas Maccabeus in Dec 164 (or Antiochus' death a short time later). When the Maccabees entered the desolated Temple, they found the altar had been profaned, the gates had been burned, and the complex overrun with weeds "as on one of the mountains" (1 Macc 4:38 NRSV). The annual celebration of the Temple's rededication became known as Hanukkah, meaning "dedication" (1 Macc 4:59); it was a holiday observed even by Christ (John 10:22).

On the other hand, interpreters of 2,300 as 1,150 days say this was the duration between Antiochus prohibiting sacrifices (sometime in 167, cf. 1 Macc 1:41–54) and the rededication of the Temple in Dec 164 (or, again, Antiochus' death). Archer suggests the distinct possibility that Antiochus banned sacrifices before he actually profaned the altar with swine.[27] Proponents of this view tie 2,300 days to the "time, times, and half times" in 7:25, but as I pointed out in the previous chapter, it's not at all clear that this phrase means 3½ years.

24. "It is with the interpretation of this chronological statement that we encounter the most disagreement about the interpretation of the symbolism of the chapter," (Longman, *Daniel*, 205).

25. So Goldingay (*Daniel*, 213), Wood (*Daniel*, 218), and Young (*Daniel*, 174–75). This is also how the LXX understands the phrase.

26. So Anderson (*Daniel*, 98), Archer ("Daniel," 103), Baldwin (*Daniel*, 158), Coffman (*Daniel*, 134), Collins (*Daniel*, 336), Lacocque (*Daniel*, 164), Montgomery (*Daniel*, 343), and Russell (*Daniel*, 151).

27. Archer, "Daniel," 103.

Finally, there is some evidence that the number is symbolic. Lucas concurs: "Attempts to find an exact chronological and historical significance for the number 2,300 have failed to provide any convincing solution. It is probably a symbolic number for a short, significant period."[28] In the end, being dogmatic over how to interpret 2,300 days overshadows the bigger point: God is sovereign over all, including the mystery of the future and the heavy hands of tyrants. He does not allow them to oppress his saints indiscriminately without restraint, but places a limit on how long they are allowed to inflict pain. He even shortens that limit in his mercy when it is his will to do so.

DANIEL WAS TOLD TO "seal up the vision" since it had to do with events in the distant future. The Hebrew verb translated "seal up" means "to stop up, make unrecognizable." Of the word's thirteen occurrences in the OT, seven have to do with stopping up or disguising water sources from an enemy since the word's root means "to hide."[29] "Applied to a book it is not strictly 'seal' but rather 'guard from use' and therefore from misuse,"[30] (cf. 8:26 NASU). Daniel's response to the vision was severe. It left him physically sick[31] for several days (which is a far cry from hitting the talk-shows or landing a seven-figure book deal), and even when he returned to work, he remained "appalled by the vision and did not understand it" (cf. 7:28).[32]

---

28. Lucas, *Daniel*, 224. Goldingay (*Daniel*, 213) points out that the numbers in 7:25; 9:24–27 are both symbolic; why would we expect the one in 8:14 to be literal?

29. NIDOTTE 3:300–301.

30. Baldwin, *Daniel*, 161.

31. Commenting on Daniel's many reactions to his visions (7:28; 8:18, 27; 10:1516), Russell says, "Such reactions are so psychologically accurate that it is tempting to see in them a reflection of the actual experience of the writer himself," (*Daniel*, 155). That is, unless these **are the experiences of the writer himself.

32. "Unfortunately Daniel was not the last person to remain bewildered by this vision after an explanation had been given!" (John J. Collins, *Daniel* [Grand Rapids: Eerdmans, 1984], 86).

Quite honestly, this last detail lends me a great deal of comfort. In our quest to fully understand the visions of Dan 7–12, we must remind ourselves often that not even Daniel understood them perfectly. I think it's OK to take our best shots at identifying vague persons such as the little horn or deciphering enigmatic phrases like "2,300 evenings and mornings." But we must never arrogantly insist our personal understanding is the correct one. Even the prophets wrote sometimes of things they did not fully understand (1 Pet 1:10–12). The best we can endeavor to do in difficult passages is to "pay attention" to "the prophetic message... as to a light shining in a dark place, until the day dawns and the morning star rises in your hearts" (2 Pet 1:19 NIV).

Elisabeth Elliot Leitch relates an occasion when she met a shepherd in Scotland who told of how he treated his sheep for insects:

> The shepherd would take his staff and run it under the horns of the ram. He then would turn the ram upside down and push his head and body under the healing water. The ram would kick and flail, trying to get away from the shepherd, but he was not strong enough. The shepherd would push him under for thirty seconds and then bring him up. The ram would be frightened, gasping for breath, still trying to get away.
>
> Then the shepherd would take his staff and push him under the healing water a second time. He wanted so desperately to be able to tell this poor little ram that everything was all right and that this was being done for his good, but such knowledge was "too wonderful" for him, past finding out (Psalm 139:6). For the ram it was just a bad day. For the shepherd it was just part of his plan to give his little ram the best.[33]

As I reflected on that story, I thought about the many things I do for

33. Rodney Stortz, *Daniel* (Wheaton, IL: Crossway, 2004), 134–35.

my baby boy that are for his own good, but that he clearly does not enjoy: baths, diaper changes, etc. My son has no clue what he really wants—let alone what he needs! Is it possible I am no different in the sight of my heavenly Father? Who am I to complain to God when I'm made to walk through dark valleys (cf. Rom 9:20–21)? If God is capable of foretelling events centuries in advance, is he then not worthy of my complete trust?

One does not have to understand all of Dan 8 to appreciate the necessity of faith in the midst of confusing and trying times. If a period of oppression should come upon the church, how will we respond? The only proper response is trust. Trust that God knows the end from the beginning, that he loves his people unconditionally, and that he is always faithful to do what is best for us. And to our trust, let us add obedience…

"For there is no other way to be happy in Jesus, but to trust and obey."

## TALKING POINTS

To confess God is in complete control of history means we must confess his sovereignty over the mightiest of earth's "movers and shakers." Alexander deservedly garnered the moniker "the Great," but Dan 8 perfectly illustrates how he was only a pawn on God's chessboard. So too was Antiochus. The first part of 8:12 contains a passive verb, "will be given over," which is another way of stating that God permitted Antiochus' reign of terror just as he had allowed Pharaoh's stubborn heart and Satan's oppression of Job. No one, not even the Prince of Darkness, can do anything without God's permission. Consider for a moment the most wicked, most powerful ruler imaginable. Even he, Scripture says, sits in the palm of God's hand. God holds his life in his hand and is able to dispense with it as he wishes. "The great horn was broken" (8:8) almost as soon as it triumphed, and the same happened to the little horn (8:25). Such is the nature of political might; it lasts only a season to accomplish the Lord's purposes, at which point the God of heaven renders judgment on evil rulers and breaks them off, making them nothing. He's the boss. That's why the second psalm closes thus: "Therefore, you kings, be wise; be warned, you rulers of the earth. Serve the LORD with fear and celebrate his rule with trembling. Kiss his son, or he will be angry and your way will lead to your destruction, for his wrath can flare up in a moment. Blessed are all who take refuge in him" (Ps 2:10-12 NIV).

It is sobering to realize that God allowed Antiochus to persecute Israel in order to purify them. Persecution is God's cleansing agent; Antiochus did not rise to power until "the transgressors [had] reached their limit" (8:23). "Because of our sins God permits such tyrants to arise and harass His church."[34] Many years before Daniel, Isaiah predicted Assyria would be God's angry rod of discipline against Israel (Isa 10:5), but

34. Young, *Daniel*, 181.

that Assyria would also be punished severely for her excessive abuse (Isa 10:15–19). Both Assyria and Antiochus were allowed by God to persecute Israel to sanctify her, but they both overstepped their bounds and were subsequently cut down by the One who had given them power.[35] The church should realize that any persecution that comes our way might be intended by God as discipline to purify and sanctify us—a realignment of our priorities (cf. Heb 12:5–11). But it is also true that the tyrant who oppresses us will also suffer God's wrath. "When such things occur, let us trust in God. The battle is His, and the overthrow of the enemy will often be without hand."[36] God is sovereign over the oppression and the oppressor.

WHEN GOD'S PEOPLE suffer, we can be sure that we are not alone in our pain. "When believers are hurt, heaven is hurt."[37] The vision of Dan 8 is ripe with reminders that there is a parallel between heaven and earth—the little horn didn't just antagonize the Jews, but also the God and the host of heaven. It reminds one of the scene in Rev 6:9–11 where the souls of the martyrs cry out, "How long?" as they witness the slaughter of their brethren. Be assured, saints, that we are not alone in our pain. God sees. God knows. God cares. Whether tribulation on a global scale or a personal level, the God of heaven feels our deepest heartaches, and his ultimate answer to our despair is Jesus (cf. John 11:33–35; Acts 9:4). On a not so distant day, Jesus will return with the armies of heaven to destroy those who persecute God's people (Rev 19:11–20; cf. 2 Thess 1:6–10) and put an end to suffering forever (Rev 21:4). Until then, it is up to us to go about the King's business as faithfully as Daniel did (Gal 6:9).

A CENTURY AND A half after the tribulation of Antiochus, Gabriel the angel made another appearance on earth. While the aged priest

35. Anderson, *Signs and Wonders*, 101.

36. Young, *Daniel*, 181.

37. Goldingay, *Daniel*, 221.

Zechariah was performing his duties in the Temple, Gabriel appeared to him with the promise of a son. This child would be "great," but not like Alexander and Antiochus, for he would be "great before the Lord" (Luke 1:15). Gabriel also appeared to Mary to announce the birth of another child. He too would be "Great," for he would be "the Son of the Most High" and ascend David's throne. In her subsequent song of praise, Mary spoke of how God "has brought down the mighty from their thrones" and "helped his servant Israel in remembrance of his mercy" (Luke 1:52, 54). Zechariah also, when John was born, prophesied that God had "raised up a horn of salvation... that we should be saved from our enemies and from the hand of all who hate us" (Luke 1:69, 71). So it is that Gabriel, who first announced to Daniel the great persecution of his people, also had a hand in announcing the advent of the One who will "kill with the breath of his mouth and bring to nothing" all powers that stand opposed to him and his people (2 Thess 2:8; cf. Ps 2:9). Hallelujah! What a Savior!

# 9

# JUST AS I AM

Yesterday, I found myself sorting through books once belonging to my dad's library. I stumbled across a small booklet I immediately recognized—a small, saddle-stitched propaganda piece with a white cover and obtrusive red letters bearing the title *88 Reasons Why the Rapture Could Be in 1988.* At the risk of spoiling the surprise, the rapture didn't happen in 1988, but this is one of many predictions made by the author, Edgar C. Whisenant, that never came true. Some of my favorites include:

- World War III was to commence on Oct 4, 1988.
- Jesus would return to earth on the Mount of Olives exactly seven years later.
- The Antichrist was born on Feb 5, 1962 at sunrise in Damascus, Syria.

As you can see, none of these things came to pass, and Mr. Whisenant was just one of a multitude of false prophets who attempted to predict the precise date of the end of all things.[1] The reason I mention this book is because much of Whisenant's reasoning was based in part on his understanding of the seventy weeks in Dan 9.

---

1. For those wondering, Whisenant claimed he was not in violation of Matt 24:36 since, at any one time, there are two days represented on the earth due to the 24 different time zones. You can't make this stuff up.

Another failed end-times prognosticator is Harold Camping. In 1992, Mr. Camping published a book alleging that 1994 would bring with it the end of all things.[2] Again, at the risk of playing the spoiler, he was wrong. But that didn't stop him from readjusting his prognostication and then saying that the end would come in 2011. Again, it didn't, and as you may have already suspected, much of Mr. Camping's reasoning came from his (mis)interpretation of Dan 9 and the seventy weeks. In fact, the Second Coming has been predicted over 200 times since World War II alone,[3] and many of those predictions have utilized Dan 9 as part of their justification. Ironically, the Talmud cursed those who used this chapter to calculate the end of time (b. *Sanhedrin* 97b).

This chapter is notoriously difficult to interpret. Everyone agrees the last four verses are the most baffling part of the chapter (and arguably the entire book), but that's where the agreement comes to a screeching halt. Montgomery is famous for calling the interpretive history of Daniel's seventy weeks "the Dismal Swamp of O.T. criticism" and a "trackless wilderness."[4] Lewis concurred: "Few biblical passages have been the subject of more speculation than has this one."[5] Even in the time of Jerome (c. A.D. 407), there was little consensus on this passage.[6]

But this does not mean the chapter is irrelevant; better yet, one does not have to understand every detail for the big picture to emerge. In fact, I believe it has been to the church's detriment that so much time and energy has been spent trying to decode this chapter without keeping in mind the big picture. This chapter is about our greatest problem, sin, and how God

---

2. Harold Camping, *1994?* (New York: Vantage, 1992). I appreciate Mr. Camping's apology in Oct 2011 that he had misled many and was abandoning further end-times prognostications.

3. Longman, *Reading the Bible*, 214–15.

4. Montgomery, *Daniel*, 400–401.

5. Lewis, *Major Prophets*, 147.

6. On the meaning of the seventy sevens, Jerome commented, "I realize that this question has been argued over in various ways by men of greatest learning, and that each of them has expressed his views according to the capacity of his own genius," (*Daniel*, 95).

planned to orchestrate our rescue. For all of its confusion, Dan 9 is a wake-up call about our need to glory in Christ for what he did in destroying the power of sin and Satan at the cross.[7]

In almost every church bulletin I read, the list of those with physical ailments seems to outnumber those with spiritual needs (the names of those with cancer alone often take up half the page). I'm not saying we shouldn't minister to those with physical ailments, or that they are not worthy of our prayers. But church, we *should* confess with Daniel that God's people have a sin problem, and that we are in need of God's great mercy. As we will learn from Daniel, our sins should grieve us deeply, our terminology should reflect their hideous nature, and whenever we are forced to say them, these words should leave behind a very bitter taste.

This chapter is not about future events from our perspective, but what God did in Christ to ransom and reconcile us back to him.[8] Also, Dan 9 relates events involving Israel and the Temple leading up to A.D. 70. Daniel wonders if either will ever be restored. He was arguably unprepared for God's answer. As you read, note the eagerness and quickness with which God revealed to Daniel those things that would take place to atone for sin. Don't miss the fact that God was more concerned with assuring Daniel that he would act for the salvation and deliverance of his people, rather than giving a precise chronological description of all that was to take place. As reflected in Daniel's prayer and Gabriel's message, God was most concerned with bringing himself glory. And only when God's people are heartbroken over sin can they properly glorify the Lord.

## DANIEL 9:1–19

Daniel's prayer and vision concerned the restoration of Jerusalem

---

7. "Total lack of self-interest and deep concern for God's name, kingdom and will characterize this prayer," (Baldwin, *Daniel*, 167).

8. "This vs. [9:24] is a Divine revelation of the fact that a definite period of time has been decreed for the accomplishment of all that which is necessary for the true restoration of God's people from bondage," (Young, *Daniel*, 195).

that began in Darius' (i.e. Cyrus; see chapter six) first year.[9] Cyrus' father is known in historical records as Cambyses I, king of Anshan, but "Ahasuerus" or "Xerxes" (NIV) may have been a royal title[10] similar to "Pharaoh." During Cyrus' first year as king, Daniel decided to study the book of Jeremiah,[11] particularly chapters 25 and 29. These passages predicted the Jews would be exiled for seventy years. Now that there had been a regime change, would the exile end and Daniel's people be allowed to return home?

At that point, Daniel began his prayer to God. His prayer was accompanied with fasting and customary grief practices such as donning sackcloth and sitting in ashes (cf. 2 Kgs 6:30; 1 Chr 21:16; Ezra 8:23; 9:3–4; Neh 9:1; Esth 4:1–3; Job 2:12; Ps 69:10; Isa 58:5; Jonah 3:5–9).[12] The prayer itself is similar to other prayers of the post-exilic period (cf. Ezra 9:6–15; Neh 1:5–11; 9:5–37; Ps 79) and is particularly saturated with language from Deuteronomy and Jeremiah. Daniel began by praising God's greatness and covenant faithfulness in spite of Israel having been unfaithful with her sin and rebellion. In fact, the covenant name of God, Yahweh, is used in the book of Daniel only in this chapter and nowhere else. In times of uncertainty, there is arguably no greater confession we can make than the fact that Yahweh is great and faithful to his people. Later in the prayer, Daniel echoed God's unparalleled greatness and faithfulness witnessed in his delivering Israel out of Egypt (9:15). He also spoke of

---

9. Turner believes this to be Darius I and a different Darius than that of Dan 5–6 (*Daniel*, 297–301), but this seems implausible since Daniel would have been almost a centenarian when Darius I began to reign.

10. D. J. Wiseman, "Some Historical Problems in the Book of Daniel" in *Notes on some problems in the Book of Daniel* (London: Tyndale, 1965), 15.

11. This proves Jeremiah's writings were already considered to be Scripture late in Daniel's lifetime, though Wilson argues that the phrase "the books" (literally, "the scrolls") only refers to Jeremiah's two letters to the exiles (Gerald H. Wilson, "The Prayer of Daniel 9: Reflection on Jeremiah 29," *JSOT* 48 [1990]: 91–99).

12. "Daniel purposefully *prepares* himself for this divine encounter... Physical preparedness and spiritual receptiveness are closely related in Scripture and indeed in our own experience of prayer," (Russell, *Daniel*, 171–72).

God's "compassion"—the actual Hebrew word used is the plural form of "womb," thereby denoting "the strong feeling of love expected within a family, especially of a mother for her child."[13]

God's people have no entitlement to his compassion or faithfulness. Like ancient Israel, we have forsaken God time and again. We have not always been obedient to the Lord, so he owes us nothing. Daniel acknowledged that Israel had gotten just what they deserved in being deported from their home. Punishment had not been instantaneous; God had sent a multitude of prophets to warn the whole nation—"our kings, our princes, and our fathers, and to all the people of the land" (9:6)—hoping they would repent, trust, and obey (cf. Neh 9:26, 34; Jer 29:19).

Solomon was right, "Sin is a reproach to any people" (Prov 14:34). Daniel poured out his pain over how Israel bore tremendous embarrassment and shame for her treatment of Yahweh. "You were right, Lord. We were wrong."[14] He acknowledged that the curses of the Law (Lev 26:14–45; Deut 28:15–68) had indeed "been poured out upon us, because we have sinned" (9:11). At any moment, the damage could have been mitigated had Israel repented and "entreated the favor of the LORD" (9:13), but they never did. God's people in every time must remember how much he hates sin. Daniel confesses, "The LORD has kept ready the calamity" (9:14). This is not in a vengeful sense, for judgment is God's alien work (Isa 28:21; cf. John 3:17). But the Father is not above disciplining his children (Heb 12:6; Rev 3:19). God does not save us so that we will feel better about our sin, but that we might learn to hate it as he does.[15]

---

13. Lucas, *Daniel*, 238.

14. "To Daniel it was more important for the God of Israel to retain his integrity and uphold his moral law than for his guilty people to escape the consequences of their infidelity," (Archer, "Daniel," 110).

15. "There is a difference between feeling miserable because sin has made our life miserable and feeling broken because our sin has offended the holiness of God and brought reproach on his name. Daniel's confession—biblical confession—is God-centered. The issue is not admitting that we have made our life miserable. The issue is admitting that there is something much worse than our misery, namely, the offended holiness and glory of God," (John Piper, "How to Pray for a

It is then that Daniel begged the Lord to relent in punishment and no longer be angry. "His prayer was a frantic, begging, pleading, prayer like the prayer of a mother whose child has just been injured and seems to be dying."[16] Jerusalem and Israel had become "a byword"—objects of ridicule among the other nations. "What a tragic confession when we consider that Israel was to be a light to all the world."[17] On the heels of the covenant curses spoken by Moses in Deut 28 had come the promise of restoration (Deut 30:2–3), and Daniel appealed to this promise in his prayer to God.

But ridicule of Israel and faithfulness to his own promise were just two parts of God's overall motive to relent and restore his people. His one singular motive was his own glory. When God had been ready to wipe out Israel in the wilderness, Moses had lobbied against it, and he had used God's glory as the reason. "What will Egypt think of you if you took Israel out of Egypt, but couldn't lead them to the Promised Land?" (Num 14:13–16). God is a jealous God in that he will not share his glory with any other (Isa 42:8; 48:11); God always acts so as to glorify himself, though we may not see it. John Piper explains:

> By punishing Israel he [God] magnified his glory by showing that idolatry is a dreadful evil worthy of destruction. ... On the other hand, since Jerusalem and Israel are "called by his name" (Dan 9:17, 18, 19), to save them and restore their prosperity after a time of punishment will magnify God's name and remove the reproach into which it has fallen among the nations (verse 16). Thus "the Lord is righteous in all his deeds" (verse 14): he has never swerved from acting for his own name's sake, even when the people have acted as if his name were worthless. When Daniel prays that Israel's deliverance accord with God's "righteous acts" (verse

Desolate Church" in *Sermons from John Piper (1990–1999)* [Minneapolis: Desiring God, 2007]).

16. Turner, *Daniel*, 314.

17. Young, *Daniel*, 186.

> 16) and that it be "for Thine own sake" (verses 17, 19), he implies that the most fundamental characteristic of divine righteousness is God's unswerving allegiance always to act for his own name's sake.[18]

## DANIEL 9:20–27

While Daniel was still praying, Gabriel came to him "at the time of the evening sacrifice" (9:21; cf. Exod 29:39), i.e. 3:00 or 4:00 pm.[19] The angel had been sent at the beginning of Daniel's prayer because the prophet was greatly loved by God (cf. Ps 139:4; Ezek 14:14, 20). Gabriel had come to give Daniel "insight and understanding"—I wish he had preserved a little more of this understanding, but it's hard to hold a grudge against a man now dead for over 2,500 years!

Gabriel announced that "seventy sevens" (Msg, NIV, cf. NLT), which most translations render as "seventy weeks," were required to accomplish six goals related to the Jews and Jerusalem (that last part is an important detail). Are these seventy literal weeks? Most interpreters say no,[20] considering the phrase to mean 490 years (cf. NCV), essentially understanding it as seventy "sabbaths." The Jews naturally thought of time in blocks of seven, somewhat similar to how we think in blocks of ten (i.e. decades). But interpreting "seventy sevens" as 490 years presents problems.

1. How are we to know this is an acceptable interpretation?
2. Are we dealing with solar years (365¼ days) or prophetic years (360 days)?

The goals of these "seventy sevens" given in 9:24 were: 1.) "to finish

---

18. John Piper, *The Justification of God*, 2nd ed. (Grand Rapids: Baker, 1993), 114.

19. Young, *Daniel*, 190.

20. The Hebrew *shabua'* means "period of seven," and is understood as a week (i.e. seven days) in Gen 29:27–28; Exod 34:22; Lev 12:5; Num 28:26; Deut 16:9–10, 16; 2 Chr 8:13; Jer 5:24; Dan 10:2–3. Still, interpreting the seventy weeks of Dan 9 as literal weeks "is almost universally rejected," (Young, *Daniel*, 196).

the transgression," 2.) "to put an end to sin," 3.) "to atone for iniquity," 4.) "to bring in everlasting righteousness," 5.) "to seal both vision and prophet, or "to confirm the prophetic vision" (NLT), and 6.) "to anoint a most holy place." These six goals were to be accomplished in the time of seventy sevens.

Gabriel divided the seventy weeks into three periods: one of seven weeks, one of 62 weeks, and then a final week. The first period of seven weeks would extend "from the going out of the word to restore and build Jerusalem" (which isn't as easy to discern as you might think) "to the coming of an anointed one, a prince." The second period of 62 weeks included the rebuilding of Jerusalem, complete with "squares and moat," meaning it would be a complete and legitimate city once again.

For the final period of one week, an anointed one would be cut off and have nothing. Then "the people of the coming prince" (9:26 HCSB) would destroy Jerusalem and its rebuilt Temple. This would come with a flood, war, and desolations. An enigmatic "he" would "make a strong covenant with many" for this final week, and "he shall put an end to sacrifice and offering. And on the wing of abominations shall come one who makes desolate, until the decreed end is poured out on the desolator" (9:27). Then Gabriel presumably disappears, the chapter ends abruptly, and we're left scratching our heads.

A few additional questions need to be considered lest the picture become muddied further.

"The word" or "decree" (HCSB) to restore Jerusalem (9:1)—is this Cyrus' decree in 539 B.C. allowing the exiles to return home (Ezra 1:1–4)? The decree of Darius I in 521 (Ezra 6:1–12)? Artaxerxes' first decree in 458 (Ezra 7:12-26) or his second to Nehemiah in 445 (Neh 2:7–8)? Others suggest "the word" points back to Jeremiah's prediction in 605 of a seventy-year exile (Jer 25:12), or to Jeremiah's promise of restoration in 586 (Jer 30:18–22; 31:38–40),[21] but none of those passages contain a

21. Thomas Edward McComiskey, "The Seventy 'Weeks' of Daniel against the Background of Ancient Near Eastern Literature," *WTJ* 47 (1985): 18–45.

decree to restore Jerusalem. According to Hag 1:4 (c. 517 B.C.), Jerusalem had already been rebuilt when Artaxerxes gave his decrees in 458 and 445. We are thus left with two interpretative options: Cyrus' decree in 539 and Darius' in 521. But they have their own problems.

Who is the "anointed one" or messiah of 9:25–26? Are there two anointed ones mentioned instead of one? I think so. The term doesn't refer to Jesus exclusively (cf. Isa 45:1)—"the terms are vaguer than the English reader might suspect"[22]—so the "anointed one" of 9:25 could be the ruler Zerubbabel or high priest Joshua who led the exiles back to Jerusalem (cf. Zech 4:14). But neither can be the anointed one of 9:26 since neither was "cut off."[23] We are thus left with two options for this second messiah-figure: Jesus or Onias, the high priest martyred during the reign of Antiochus (2 Macc 4:30–34). I believe Jesus is the "anointed one" in 9:26; the martyrdom of Onias accomplished none of the six goals mentioned in 9:24.

Who are the people of the prince who destroy Jerusalem and the Temple (9:26)? Is this the same prince as the one mentioned in the previous verse, one who was said to be an anointed one? Some say this passage points to the time of Antiochus, as does the prophecy of Dan 8, 11.[24] But Jerusalem was never destroyed during Antiochus' reign, and the Temple was only defiled. Plus, as stated above, the entire period of Antiochus' reign did not accomplish the goals of the seventy sevens laid out in 9:24, so we must be dealing with some other period in history.[25]

Other questions are just as important: Are the seventy weeks contiguous, or are there "prophetic gaps" in between? Premillennial

22. Baldwin, *Daniel*, 170.

23. Young (*Daniel*, 206) points out that this phrase "in the present passage ... means 'cut off by death,'" (cf. Lev 7:20; Ps 37:9).

24. So Montgomery, who then calls the seventy weeks "a chronological miscalculation on part of the writer," (*Daniel*, 393). Such a judgment is unnecessary if the seventy weeks 1.) do not concern Antiochus, and 2.) are not meant to be chronological.

25. If you want to know how I really feel, I consider imposing the period of Antiochus onto this passage to be an irresponsible handling of the text in the worst way. It just doesn't fit.

interpreters claim such a gap between the 69th and 70th week. This "gap" began in the time of Christ and continues until the beginning of the seven-year Great Tribulation. Against this view, it is rightly argued that every other prophesied period in Scripture is understood to be contiguous or consecutive—Joseph's seven consecutive years of famine, 430 consecutive years of Egyptian slavery, forty consecutive years of wilderness wandering—so how and why would one naturally assume an unprecedented "prophetic gap" in Dan 9 when such is not expressly spelled out for us?[26]

What was the "strong covenant" and "wing of abominations" (9:27)? Young's interpretations seem to make the most sense. The ambiguous "he" who makes a "strong covenant" in 9:27 is a reference to Jesus and how he *fulfilled* (cf. "confirm," KJV) the covenant—the same word is used in Ps 12:4 in the sense of "prevail." The Hebrew phrase so often translated "to make a covenant" (e.g. Gen 15:18; Exod 34:10; Deut 5:2) does not occur here, so something else must be in view. This proposal is strengthened by the statement that this "he" will "put an end to sacrifice and offering," meaning the entire sacrificial system. This is exactly what Jesus accomplished with the atonement (cf. Eph 2:14–15; Col 2:14–17; Heb 10:11–14). "When Christ was put to death on the cross, there was no rightful place ever for another single animal sacrifice or oblation."[27]

As for the "wing of abomination," the phrase itself (not to mention the entire verse) is notoriously difficult to translate. It's likely a reference to the pinnacle of the Temple;[28] in a veiled way, God was predicting the Temple's total destruction, "inasmuch as the capture of the highest part

26. Hasel calls the seventy weeks "a complete and uninterrupted span of time." Arguing on the basis of Hebrew grammar and syntax, he concludes, "It is a given that the period of 'seventy weeks' is limited in chronological time and cannot be stretched into something indefinite in historical time," (Gerhard F. Hasel, "The Hebrew Masculine Plural for 'Weeks' in the Expression 'Seventy Weeks' in Daniel 9:24," *AUSS* 31 [1993]: 105–18).

27. Turner, *Daniel*, 334.

28. Young, *Daniel*, 218.

presupposes the possession of all the rest."[29]

Hopefully, you by now see why this chapter has been so divisive among interpreters. Smarter people than I have wrestled with this passage, only to come up empty on an interpretation that satisfies everyone, so I'm not about to pretend I hold the golden key that unlocks all its mysteries. The most I can do is offer up some ideas and attempt to share with you what I believe is the big picture, lest we get bogged down in details.

Hailey points out that "symbols abound in Daniel's visions," and that it's unwise to force a literal interpretation on the seventy weeks.[30] I agree. Regardless of the date you pick to begin the seventy weeks, none terminates at both a conclusive and meaningful date.[31] It's beyond me as to why some symbolically interpret "seventy weeks" as 490 years, but then become dogmatic about it being 490 literal years, rather than understanding the phrase's full symbolic meaning.

It may surprise you to learn that, no matter how you reckon the years Israel spent in exile, the final tally never comes out to seventy. In Zech 1:12, the seventy years of exile were considered still ongoing, and this was in 519 B.C.! In Lev 26:18, Moses had warned Israel would be punished "sevenfold" (an obviously symbolic term) for her sins (cf. Lev 26:21), which leads me to believe we are also intended to interpret the seventy years of exile symbolically, namely as the perfect work of God to punish and restore his

29. E. W. Hengstenberg, *Christology of the Old Testament*, vol. 3 (Grand Rapids: Kregel, 1956), 149. "This prophecy centres not on restoring and building Jerusalem, but on the one who will devastate it," (Lucas, *Daniel*, 243).

30. Hailey, *Daniel*, 181.

31. Some argue that starting with Artaxerxes' decree to Ezra (457 B.C.) brings one to A.D. 32, the year of Jesus' crucifixion. But already in Ezra's day, Jerusalem and the Temple had been restored (it only lacked walls), and we don't know for certain which year Jesus was crucified. Since the NT never makes explicit reference to the seventy sevens, at least chronologically, I concur with Longman: "Attempts to correlate these years, understood as 490 years … have been unpersuasive to any but a few devoted followers. Such futile efforts work against the purpose of these texts, which is to point to God's determined timing of the end of sin and suffering without revealing the exact timing," (*Daniel*, 229; cf. Lewis, *Major Prophets*, 147).

people.[32] In the same way, seventy sevens (i.e. 70 x 7) represents God's "perfect upon perfect" timing to bring Jesus into the world.

We must remember that the OT prophets' role was to point the way to Christ (Luke 24:44; 1 Pet 1:10–12). Particularly relevant here is Peter's comment that the prophets wanted to know about "the sufferings of Christ and subsequent glories" (1 Pet 1:11). Only after Jesus do we read that "the mystery" of the "prophetic writings" had been revealed (Rom 16:25). To the Ephesians, Paul spoke of God's mystery "set forth in Christ as a plan for the fullness of time" (Eph 1:9–10); in Colossians, he wrote of a "mystery hidden for ages ... now revealed to his saints ... which is Christ in you, the hope of glory" (Col 1:26–27; cf. 2:2; 4:3). In this way, Jesus sealed "vision and prophecy" (9:24 NASU), meaning he validated all that the prophets had predicted and been pointing to in their preaching[33] (cf. 2 Cor 1:20; Heb 1:1–2).

For all the murky confusion surrounding the seventy sevens, the NT is clear that Jesus "put an end to sin," meaning he broke its power at the cross and reconciled us back to God (Rom 5:6–10; cf. Heb 9:26). As the Righteous One (Acts 3:14), he atoned for iniquity (Heb 2:17; 7:23–8:6; 10:1–14) by offering himself up as a propitiation for our sins (Rom 3:25; 1 John 2:2) and ushering in "everlasting righteousness" (1 Cor 1:30; 2 Cor 5:21). The only way God's people can lay claim to everlasting righteous is by being "made right" by our faith in this Righteous One (Rom 3:23-26).

Consequently, we now can enter a new "most holy place" (Heb 10:19) since it is in our hearts—"Christ in you, the hope of glory!" Two

32. William Foxwell Albright concluded that seventy years "was a recognized pattern for the period of destruction of cities or countries whose gods still remained interested in their people," (*From the Stone Age to Christianity*, 2nd ed. [Garden City, NJ: Doubleday, 1957], 18). "The period suggests that the seventy years of punishment due according to Jer 25:11/29:10 is being exacted sevenfold in accordance with Lev 26," (Goldingay, *Daniel*, 257).

33. Longman, *Daniel*, 226. Contra Young, who argues, "The reference is not to accrediting the prophecy, but to sealing it up so that it will no longer appear. Its functions are finished, and it is not henceforth needed," (*Daniel*, 200). But if you think about it, these two interpretations are just two sides of the same coin.

Greek words are used in the NT to refer to the Temple—the *hieron* (the Temple complex, e.g. Matt 21:12) and the *naos* (the actual Most Holy Place, e.g. Matt 27:51). It is this last term that Paul uses in 1 Cor 6:19. Our bodies are the new *naos*, the Most Holy Place of the Spirit, and the Spirit's indwelling was made possible by the atoning sacrifice of Jesus (cf. Acts 2:38; Rom 8:9–11). By virtue of the Spirit's indwelling, transgression is restricted (cf. Gal 5:16; Eph 3:16; 1 John 3:6).

The final two verses of Dan 9 allude to the destruction of Jerusalem and the Temple, which occurred in A.D. 70 at the hands of the Romans. Jesus himself had foreseen this terrible event and declared it to be God's punishment of Israel for having rejected Jesus as the anointed one (Luke 19:41–44; 1 Thess 2:14–16; cf. Amos 3:6). On another occasion, our Lord recalled "the abomination of desolation spoken of by the prophet Daniel" (Matt 24:15) and warned his followers in Judea to "flee to the mountains" that they might be spared.

The abominations mentioned by Daniel and Christ included the presence of the pagan Roman military, as well as acts of murder by the Zealots and the installation of an illegitimate high priest (Josephus, *Wars* 4.3.6–8, 10; 4.5.4). After a siege of just a few months in Spring 70, Rome dismantled Jerusalem under the leadership of General Titus as if it were made of Legos. The Romans desecrated the Most Holy Place by offering pagan sacrifices there (*Wars* 6.316). Titus ordered only three towers and part of the western wall be left standing "to demonstrate to posterity what kind of city it was," (*Wars* 7.1.1–2). So total was this destruction that Josephus was forced to concede, "Daniel also wrote concerning the Roman government, and that our country should be made desolate by them," (*Antiquities* 10.276). Titus returned to Rome with nearly 100,000 POWs (*Wars* 6.420),[34] and Judaism hasn't been the same since.

---

34. Josephus puts the total death toll of the Jewish War at over a million. As a historian, Josephus is known to have grossly exaggerated numbers, but even if that number is not correct, it still testifies to the great judgment that came upon the Jews some forty years after the execution of the Messiah.

But the Christians in Jerusalem escaped this fate. The church historian Eusebius records how they, "commanded by revelation," escaped the city two years before its fall for the town of Pella. Only then, Eusebius says, did God's judgment overtake "those who had committed such outrages against Christ and his apostles, and totally destroyed that generation of impious men," (*Hist. eccl.* 3.5.3). In other words, all of this happened because the Jews refused to kiss the Son and take refuge in him (Ps 2:12).

Behold, the derision of heaven.

We would be remiss if we ignored the final statement of Dan 9, that a "decreed end" would come on those who destroyed Jerusalem and the Temple. God used Rome to judge Israel just as he had also used Assyria and Babylon. But his wrath also turned on Assyria and Babylon, and it also turned on Rome. This has been a recurring theme in the book of Daniel, that God has fixed the times of all nations and empires. Only the kingdom of God will stand forever. So sure is he that such will happen that he is willing to declare it; once God has declared something, it must happen, for his word does not return to him empty (Isa 55:11).

To summarize, I believe the seventy weeks are not to be interpreted literally as 490 years or any other chronological number, but symbolically as God's "fullness of time" (Gal 4:4) in which he brought Christ into the world.[35] The coming of Jesus was to atone for sin (Heb 2:17; 1 John 4:10) and establish his kingdom (Matt 16:18), not on earth (John 18:36), but in the hearts of his people (Luke 17:21), the new Most Holy Place of God (1 Cor 6:19). Thus, we can say with Mauro, "When our Lord ascended into heaven and the Holy Spirit descended, there remained not one of the

35. "It appears that the principal emphasis is not upon the beginning and ending of this remarkable period but upon the mighty events which were to transpire therein, events which have wrought our peace with God. The passage is Messianic through and through. Well will it be for us, if we too, in our study of this supremely important prophecy, place our emphasis, no upon dates and mathematical calculations, but upon the central Figure who was both anointed and a prince, who by being cut off has made reconciliation for iniquity and brought in the only righteousness that is acceptable with God, even His own eternal righteousness," (Young, *Daniel*, 221).

six items of Daniel 9:24 that was not *fully accomplished*."[36]

ONE OF MY FAVORITE gospel hymns is Bill and Gloria Gaither's "Because He Lives." The second verse gained new meaning for me when I first held my son in my arms only moments after his birth. I've held him many occasions since, and every time I do, I "feel the pride, and joy he gives / but greater still the calm assurance / this child can face uncertain days because He lives." Another hymn that has always moved me, "Just As I Am," has a final verse that says, "Just as I am / Thy love unknown / has broken every barrier down / Now to be Thine, yea, Thine alone."

I don't know what the future holds for my family or for me, just as Daniel did not know the fate of his people as the exile came to an end. But he provides for us an excellent model to imitate in that he searched the Scriptures and sought the mercy of God in prayer. You and I can face uncertain times because Jesus lived, died, and rose again; because we are God's and God's alone. We can face a turbulent future because Jesus overcame our greatest problem—sin—with his sacrifice. And Jesus lives to remind us that we, like Daniel, are greatly beloved by God.

36. Philip Mauro, *The Seventy Weeks and the Great Tribulation* (Boston: Hamilton, 1923), 53. Archer believers all or most of the six goals still await fulfillment ("Daniel," 113).

## TALKING POINTS

My heart is warmed at the thought of Daniel praying, not only for his contemporaries, but also for all the people of God who followed him. The visions that took place centuries after Daniel's lifetime caused the old prophet to pray fervently for the church in years to come. Like Ezekiel, he identified with God's people when they suffered (cf. Ezek 3:14–15). The church today has the same obligation to pray for all saints everywhere and in every time. Jesus himself did this on the eve of his death. Like Daniel, let us pray that God will continue to forgive the church's sin, that he will comfort and strengthen us, that he will keep us bold and courageous, but also humble and submissive. Let us pray that our children and grandchildren are given the strength from above to withstand the persecution of tomorrow. Let us pray that they, like Daniel and his friends, are granted God's wisdom to understand the times and know what the church should do. Above all, let us pray as Jesus did that those after us will be one in Christ so that the world will believe on him, even as they put his servants to death (John 17:21). Let us pray that Christ is glorified always, whether in life or in death (Phil 1:20).

I wish I could say the Lord's people no longer bring reproach on him, but that wouldn't be an honest statement. I heard the statement once that some will go to hell because they never knew a Christian, and others will go because they *did* know a Christian. It bothers me that the sins of the world seem to make us more indignant than our own. Jesus called that hypocrisy (Matt 7:3–5). As the church enters a form of exile in the U.S., we need to be convicted once again of the need to be Christ-like in our attitude and actions. Though it's important to be ready to give an answer, we are commanded to do so "with gentleness and respect" (1 Pet 3:15). Few will be asking about our hope in the first place if they are not witnessing in us a shining light of the Spirit's fruit (Gal 5:22–23). To that end, God's people must follow Daniel's example by rededicating themselves to daily Bible study. I'm not talking about a five-minute devotional skimming of Psalms before bed, but in-depth study of the whole counsel of God like a starving, homeless man ushered into a banquet hall for a sumptuous Thanksgiving feast. To such study, we must also add fervent prayer in which we humbly confess sin, declare God's glory, and seek his will. We will find, as was the case with Daniel, that our words lift themselves from the pages of Scripture and become the expression of our heart as we enter his presence to "receive mercy and find grace to help in time of need" (Heb 4:16; cf. John 15:7).

# 10

## THE REST OF THE STORY

When I was ten, I started listening to Paul Harvey's *The Rest of the Story*. It was riveting to hear the background of people, things, or events now famous—the childhood of W. C. Fields, the origin of Coke and the potato chip, or how Stevie Wonder developed his keen sense of hearing. These accounts from the famous radio personality were a reminder that there are always details unknown to us. It's easy to believe we know all the facts, but Harvey's surprise twist and signature sign-off exposed our ignorance: "And now you know the rest of the story."

In some ways, Daniel learned "the rest of the story" in a way he did not expect. Not only was he told about future events, but he was also given a glimpse behind the curtain that shrouds the spiritual realm from us mortals. At the time of this final vision, Daniel was in his late 80s, and the experience exacted a physical toll on his body. Only after being strengthened by a mysterious figure was Daniel capable of receiving the vision.

Wouldn't it be nice if we knew "the rest of the story" of our lives? Or even better, how great would it be if we had perfect knowledge of what was going on in heaven parallel to our earthly circumstances? Hypothetically, if we knew an answer to our prayers was being delayed by the demon assigned to the Iranians, would we be more or less encouraged? If Job had known why he was being made to suffer, would it have made it easier for him?

In this final section of Daniel, the aged prophet was given a very specific, detailed glimpse at the future of his people. He learned that difficult hardship awaited them, but that Daniel personally would die in peace and be resurrected with the rest of God's saints. Yet, after reading the effect this all had on Daniel, I doubt I want to know too much about the future. As soon as we think we can predict future events, a twist occurs that no one expected. As early as high school, we plan out our whole lives, but they almost never go that way. Could there be more to life than always knowing what's about to happen next?

In chapter 7, I mentioned how apocalyptic literature may be meant by God to arouse our emotions. With such a specific prophecy as the one we find here, it is easy to (mis)use it to map out the future. Such is technically possible since God decreed that it would happen, and we know none of his words fall to the ground. But it misses the point to use apocalyptic passages to predict the future. Such portions of Scripture are meant to arouse in us an abiding faith in God's sovereignty and inspire us to trust him completely with everything, especially the future. If God is capable of accurately foretelling both the events of tomorrow and those a hundred years from now, then he is worthy of our trust, no matter the circumstances.

I've often heard religion lampooned as a crutch for the weak, but for those who know they're lame, a crutch is rather handy. We don't always know what is going on in the spiritual realm. Truth be told, there are some things we probably don't want to know. Nor are we equipped to know the entire future. In such a state, we are "crippled." That's why I believe the best course is to trust and obey God. He alone knows "the rest of the story."

## DANIEL 10

A final vision came to Daniel in Cyrus' third year (536 B.C.), and it would prove to be a massive one, characterized by some of the most specific predictions in Scripture. "The word was true, and it was a great conflict" (10:1), meaning this vision was a reliable one concerning a major war in both the spiritual and physical realms. When the vision came, Daniel had been fasting and praying for three weeks.[1] He had suspended the use of lotions, which were applied in hot, dry climates as a sort of deodorant;[2] thus, they were not used during times of mourning (cf. 2 Sam 12:20; 14:2; Ps 45:7; Eccl 9:8; Isa 61:3; Amos 6:6). Daniel grieved as one would for the dead, sin, or calamity (cf. Gen 37:34; Ezra 10:6; Ezek 7:12). The reason for his grief may have been Daniel's premonition of the difficulties facing the Jews in Jerusalem.[3] The foundation of the second Temple would be laid in April 536, but the project would be quickly suspended due to the Samaritans' intense opposition (Ezra 3:8, 10; 4:4–5).

A couple of days before, on Nisan 24 (early April),[4] Daniel saw a "man" standing on the banks of the Tigris River. The description of this "man" (10:5–6) is a majestic one (cf. Ezek 1:5–28). Fine clothes such as a priest would wear (Exod 28:42; Lev 6:10; 16:4), a golden belt,[5] a body of beryl (a yellowish gemstone thought to have come from Spain; cf. "topaz," NIV), a face like lightening, eyes like torches, limbs like bronze, and a voice like a stadium crowd—this is almost identical to the description of Jesus that John gave (Rev 1:13–15), and as we will see, Daniel's reaction to seeing this "man" was identical to John's (Rev 1:17). Only Daniel could see this "man," but his companions were frightened nonetheless and ran away (cf. Acts 9:7). We are thus left with the image of Daniel fainting facedown as if paralyzed with fear.

Daniel was revived and helped to his hands and knees (cf. Ezek 1:28–2:2). This mysterious "man" bade him to stand since he had been sent

1. "Daniel made his body feel as his soul felt. This harmony of the external with the internal state was conducive to earnest prayer," (Leupold, *Daniel*, 445).

2. Jerome reports that, in his day, application of lotion replaced daily baths in Persia and India (*Daniel*, 111).

3. William H. Shea, "Wrestling with the Prince of Persia: A Study of Daniel 10," *AUSS* 21 (1983): 225–50.

4. This date is significant, indicating Passover had been observed during Daniel's fast, and that the prophet would have reflected on Israel's bitter suffering in Egypt (cf. Exod 12; Deut 16:3).

5. The text says this belt was made "of fine gold from Uphaz" as if Uphaz is a place. "No such place, however, is known," (Young, *Daniel*, 225).

to inform Daniel of why his prayer had not been answered. This divine messenger had been dispatched to answer Daniel's petition as soon as he had begun praying (cf. 9:23), but "the prince of the Persian kingdom" (10:13 NIV) had resisted this messenger and delayed him for three weeks. We aren't told specifically how or why the delay was successful, but this prince may have been behind the earthly opposition to the Temple's restoration. The divine messenger had appeared now only because Michael, the guardian archangel of Israel, had come to his aid. The dark powers knew if his mission was successful, not only would Daniel (also Israel and the church) be encouraged by the vision, but once the vision was delivered, the events were sure to come to pass, for "the declaration of God's intention means its implementation."[6]

Twice in this passage, Daniel is said to be "greatly loved" (10:11, 19) by God.[7] But whether due to his advanced age, his recent fast, or the intensity of this vision (arguably a little of all these), Daniel complained it was too much for him—"pain" (10:16) is also used in the OT for that of childbirth (1 Sam 4:19; Isa 13:8; 21:3). One like "the children of men" called Daniel to have courage and touched him on the lips (cf. Isa 6:6–7; Jer 1:9) to strengthen him. Now prepared both spiritually *and* physically to receive the vision, Daniel was told "the rest of the story." He was given a startling peek behind the curtain into the spiritual realm. This "man" informed Daniel that he was returning to the fray against the prince of Persia and prince of Greece with only Michael as his comrade-in-arms.

Who is this "man" in Dan 10? As mentioned before, some take him to be the pre-incarnate Christ. The parallels between his appearance in Dan 10 and the vision of Jesus in Rev 1 are too striking to ignore. This figure certainly inspired more terror in Daniel than did Gabriel; he "is more

---

6. Lucas, *Daniel*, 276.

7. Baldwin excellently observes that few in Scripture are complimented as well as Daniel is here. She mentions Abraham (2 Chr 20:7; Isa 41:8; Jas 2:23), Mary (Luke 1:28, 30), and Christ (Isa 42:1; Matt 3:17), but concludes, "For each of these people suffering was inescapable," (*Daniel*, 180–81).

radiant than Gabriel and greater than Michael."[8] Identifying this divine messenger with God would explain why his appearance affected Daniel as it did (cf. Exod 33:20). The Lord often appeared to his servants in human form at pivotal moments in the scheme of redemption (e.g. Gen 18:1; 32:24; Josh 5:13–15; Isa 6:1; John 12:41). "To the two Jewish exiles—Daniel in Babylon and the Apostle John on Patmos—Jesus appeared as the glorified King-Priest. After seeing the Son of God, both men were given visions of future events that involved the people of God, events that would be difficult to accept and understand."[9]

Yet a common and sound argument against this view is, how could this "man" be Christ if he required Michael to reinforce him? The argument is void if we see two persons in this passage—the first being Christ and the second being an angel (Gabriel?), but I personally don't see room for two figures, only one. I think we are to see this mysterious figure as the pre-incarnate Christ,[10] but along with Longman,[11] I'm reticent to be dogmatic about any of this since his identity is left ambiguous.

Before we move onto the vision given in Dan 11–12, how are we to interpret the mysterious reference to the princes of Persia and Greece? When Satan was cast from heaven, he took with him fallen angels (2 Pet 2:4; Jude 6), known as demons in the NT. God assigned angels to the various nations of the earth (cf. Deut 32:8; Heb 2:5), so it seems reasonable to conclude that Satan did the same thing. These fallen angels became the false gods of the nations (cf. Ps 106:37–38; 1 Cor 10:20). In other words, the princes of Persia and Greece with whom Michael and this "man" were doing battle were actually gods or demons under the

8. Ibid., 178. "What we have in these verses is something far more awesome than a mere angelic being," (Anderson, *Signs and Wonders*, 122).

9. Wiersbe, *Be Resolute*, 123.

10. Alternative suggestions include Gabriel (Montgomery, *Daniel*, 420) or some other angel other than Gabriel or Michael (Wood, *Daniel*, 268). See Gillian Bampfylde, "The Prince of the Host in the Book of Daniel and the Dead Sea Scrolls," *JSJ* 14 (1983): 129–34.

11. Longman, *Daniel*, 250.

command of Satan (cf. Eph 6:12; Rev 12:7). These demons were not restricted by geographical boundaries—"the 'princes' are over the *people* of Persia and Greece and their *sociopolitical structure* rather than their respective geographical boundaries."[12] If it's true that the whole world lies under Satan's control (1 John 5:19; cf. John 14:30; 2 Cor 4:4; Eph 2:2), it's not a stretch to believe he also enjoys tremendous influence over earthly governments.

This passage evidences the parallel between events on earth and in heaven (cf. Num 10:35–36; Judg 5:19–20; Isa 24:21).[13] Two OT stories illustrate this perfectly. The first is when Elisha and his servant awakened one morning to find an Aramean detachment had surrounded them. While Elisha was cool, calm, and collected, the servant was ready to hit the panic button, but Elisha prayed that God would open his servant's eyes to the angelic armies arrayed against the Arameans (2 Kgs 6:15–23). The other, of course, is the story of Job's suffering. Not once was this good man told of the heavenly events of Job 1–2, that his suffering had a parallel in the spiritual realm. Christ believed in a spiritual/physical parallel, and at times made cryptic references to it (e.g. Luke 10:18; 11:21–22).

Apparently, a struggle had been taking place in the spiritual realm between the angels and the demon of Persia, perhaps for the soul of Cyrus around the time he allowed the Jews to return to Jerusalem[14] (cf. 11:1; Ezra 1:1). It wouldn't be long before this struggle would also involve the demon of Greece; much of Dan 11 concerns Israel during the days of the Greek Empire. Bizarre as it sounds, the divine messenger in Dan 10 seemed thankful for Daniel's persistent prayer since only Michael was by

12. David E. Stevens, "Daniel 10 and the Notion of Territorial Spirits," *BibSac* 157 (2000): 427–28. He argues that these demons "are better termed 'empire spirits' rather than territorial spirits," (Ibid., 428).

13. When God judges a nation, he also judges the gods or fallen angels in charge of that nation (Exod 12:12; Num 33:4; Jer 46:25; 1 Cor 8:5).

14. "Knowing that such a development could lead to the ultimate appearance of the Son of God as the Messiah for God's redeemed, Satan and all his hosts were determined to thwart the renewal of Israel and the deliverance of her people from destruction," (Archer, "Daniel," 127).

the messenger's side (cf. Jas 5:16). "It is as if he wanted Daniel to enter a solemn pact to continue praying while the heavenly conflict lasted, because he had no other support."[15] Paul was adamant that the church's war is not with physical powers, but with evil spiritual powers (Eph 6:12); the armor and weapons of this war belong not to the world (2 Cor 10:3–4), but to God: truth, righteousness, faith, salvation, the gospel, and the Word (Eph 6:14–17). Paul then exhorted us to wage spiritual warfare by "praying at all times in the Spirit, with all prayer and supplication. To that end keep alert with all perseverance, making supplication for all the saints" (Eph 6:18; cf. Luke 18:1).

Having encouraged Daniel, the messenger commenced to relate to the prophet "what is inscribed in the book of truth" (10:21; cf. Ps 139:16). "In the ancient world that which was written was taken far more seriously than that which was spoken. The 'writing of truth' points to God's foreknowledge of future events. That which God foreknows will certainly take place. He is not, therefore, embarrassed to put down in writing his revelations."[16]

## DANIEL 11

The prophecy of this chapter is startling in its detail and accuracy; some 130 predictions are made in the first 35 verses. The chapter is without rival or precedent in the rest of the OT. Nowhere else is so much specific, predictive prophecy to be found in one place, and the acid test of whether prophecy is from God is if it comes to pass (Deut 18:20–22). The fact that this passage is so specific *and* accurate leads some scholars to conclude it was the work of a historian, rather than a prophet inspired by God who

---

15. Wallace, *The Lord Is King*, 179. The efficacy of Daniel's petitions remind me of Mary Queen of Scots and how she supposedly feared the prayers of John Knox more than a foreign invader. "Such power is itself an encouragement to pray," (Ferguson, *Daniel*, 217).

16. James E. Smith, *The Major Prophets* (Joplin, MO: College Press, 1992), 619; cf. Baldwin, *Daniel*, 282; Keil, *Daniel*, 423.

knows the end from the beginning.[17] The chapter describes more than 400 years of events that lay in the future from Daniel's perspective; it reads like a historical survey of the period with only the names and dates missing.

At the outset of the chapter, the divine messenger passes over 200 years of Persian history, but not without mentioning a fourth king,[18] Xerxes I, who was indeed very wealthy (cf. Esth 1) and launched a campaign against Greece in 480 B.C. He was slowed considerably by the courageous 300 Spartans at Thermopylae, and then defeated at Salamis, Plataea, and Mycale (cf. 11:2).[19] The remaining Persian kings are skipped over in Dan 11 without mention; during their reigns, Persia and Greece were at odds with one another until the rise of Alexander the Great in 336. Alexander's rule would be short-lived, ending in 323 almost as soon as it had begun (cf. 11:3–4). Within a few years after his death, Alexander's mentally challenged half-brother, Phillip III, his young son, Alexander IV, and his prime minister, Perdiccas, were all assassinated, leaving no undisputed heir.

Alexander's empire was eventually divided among four of his generals; the two with relevance to Israel were Seleucus I in Syria ("the king of the north") and Ptolemy I in Egypt ("the king of the south").[20] Seleucus initially was met with hostility by another of Alexander's generals, Antigonus I, and was forced to seek asylum in Egypt under Ptolemy. This made Seleucus one of Ptolemy's "princes" for about four years before defeating Antigonus

---

17. "Human thought, enthroned, has judged a chapter such as Daniel 11 to be history written after the event, whereas God enthroned, the one who was present at the beginning of time and will be present when time is no more, may surely claim with justification to 'announce from of old the things to come' (Isa. 44:7)," (Baldwin, *Daniel*, 185).

18. The three previous Persian kings have traditionally been identified as Cambyses, Smerdis, and Darius I.

19. Coffman (*Daniel*, 167) makes a valid point when he says, if Dan 11 is history passed off as predictive prophecy, why was Xerxes' campaign against Greece and the Maccabean revolt both passed over in this chapter with little or no comment?

20. "The reason that the other two kingdoms do not here appear upon the page of prophecy is thus made clear. The angel told Daniel he was going to show him what should befall *his* people; and those two kingdoms had no place in connection with Israel or their land," (Ironside, *Daniel*, 195–96).

at Gaza, regaining control over Syria, and thus he became "stronger than" Ptolemy (11:5).[21] About 75 years after Alexander's death, Ptolemy II[22] offered a peace treaty to the Seleucid ruler, Antiochus II, in the form of his (Ptolemy's) daughter Berenice's hand in marriage. But for this to work, Antiochus had to divorce his current wife and disinherit their two sons. He did so, but was reconciled to Laodice two years later, only for Laodice to poison Antiochus and arrange for her son, Seleucus II, to murder Berenice and her baby (cf. 11:6). Seleucus then inherited the throne.

Before the deaths of Antiochus and Berenice, Ptolemy II (Berenice's father) had died, bringing Ptolemy III to power. He avenged his sister's assassination by invading Syria and seizing the capital, Antioch. Ptolemy returned from Syria with much plunder, including 40,000 talents of silver and 2,500 idols,[23] some of which had first been stolen by the Persian king Cambyses when he had captured Egypt in 524 (cf. 11:7–8). In 242, Seleucus II retaliated with an invasion of Egypt, but was forced to retreat very quickly (11:9). In 217, Antiochus III met Ptolemy IV in battle at Raphia, and Ptolemy was victorious, suffering only 2,200 casualties to Antiochus' 17,000 (Polybius, *Histories* 5.79). Palestine subsequently came under the dominion of the Ptolemies (cf. 11:11–12).

Ptolemy IV died under suspicious circumstances in 203 (he was only in his thirties). Since Ptolemy V was just six at the time, Agathocles the prime minister was the true ruler, but he became very unpopular. Antiochus III and Philip V of Macedon exploited the crisis by defeating the Egyptians at Gaza and Paneas in 200. These victories reclaimed Palestine for the Seleucids (11:13). After the battle at Paneas, the Egyptians retreated to the fortress-city of Sidon on the Mediterranean coast, but Antiochus III besieged it and was victorious in 198, further strengthening his hold of "the glorious land," i.e. Palestine (cf. 11:15–16;

21. Seleucus' territory was much larger than Ptolemy's, stretching from Asia Minor in the west to the Indus River in the east.

22. The LXX was translated in Alexandria, Egypt during the reign of Ptolemy II.

23. Jerome, *Daniel*, 123.

Polybius, *Histories* 16.18; 28.1). Meanwhile in the West, Rome was slowly growing in its power. To fortify himself against this new enemy, Antiochus III allied with the Ptolemies by giving his daughter, Cleopatra I, as a wife to Ptolemy V, who was only sixteen at the time. The ploy backfired, however, when Cleopatra (who evidently wasn't much of a daddy's girl) convinced her husband to ally with Rome against her father (cf. 11:17).

At the encouragement of the famous Hannibal, Antiochus III attacked Rome-protected Greece and his old friend Phillip V in 192. But under the command of Lucius Scipio Asiaticus, the Romans defeated Antiochus at Thermopylae in 191 and again at Magnesia in 190, the latter being a crushing blow to Antiochus (his force of 70,000 was defeated by Rome's 30,000). In 189, he signed a treaty with Rome at Apamea that required him to forfeit twenty hostages (one of them being Antiochus' son, Antiochus IV), submit to Rome's authority as a vassal king, and pay a rather large tribute or indemnity for being such a huge headache. This last requirement left Antiochus flat broke. He was also ordered to never again venture west of the Taurus Mountains. Two years later, Antiochus was assassinated for plundering a temple in Persia in an effort to pay his bill to Rome (cf. 11:18–19).

Seleucus IV inherited the throne when Antiochus III died, and he sent Heliodorus, the prime minister, to Jerusalem to plunder its Temple treasury for funds to pay the Romans their annual tribute of a thousand talents (11:20), but according to 2 Macc 3:7–40, a dream scared Seleucus into backing down. Seleucus did not reign long, nor did he die gloriously "with his boots on,"[24] but was poisoned in 175 by Heliodorus. Seleucus' brother, Antiochus IV, was returning from Rome and was in Athens when the assassination took place, but he still may have been involved in the conspiracy. This, then, is how the infamous Antiochus IV rose to power.[25] He was indeed "a contemptible person," and "royal majesty" (11:21)

24. Montgomery, *Daniel*, 445.

25. In this passage, "the ruler in question is Antiochus Epiphanes, and on this there is no disagreement," (Baldwin, *Daniel*, 183).

technically did not belong to him since Seleucus' son, Demetrius, was the rightful heir to the throne.[26] We already know Antiochus was a master of intrigue (8:23); here, we learn that he seized his throne "by flatteries." Antiochus was known to give more lavish gifts to his supporters compared to his predecessors (1 Macc 3:30).

Since the time of Artaxerxes, "the Torah had been the law of the land in Judea,"[27] and it had been customary to allow the Jews to govern themselves with the high priest ("the prince of the covenant," 11:22) in charge (cf. Ezra 7). Onias III was high priest in Jerusalem when Antiochus became king. Antiochus was driven to spread Greek culture as far and wide as possible. Onias' brother, Jason, offered Antiochus a bribe and a promise of supporting the Hellenization of Judaism in exchange for being named the high priest. Antiochus agreed, deposed Onias in 175, and installed Jason as high priest (2 Macc 4:7–10). But a man named Menelaus, not even of the tribe of Levi, offered Antiochus a bigger bribe and was made high priest in place of Jason. Installing a high priest without the proper ancestry was an unthinkable act in Judaism.[28] After accusing Menelaus of stealing golden vessels from the Temple, Onias fled for his life, but was assassinated by Menelaus (2 Macc 4:30–34).

In 170, Antiochus attacked Ptolemy VI and defeated him at Pelusium; in the aftermath, he also captured Memphis and much of the rest of Egypt. Two of Ptolemy's advisors, Eulaeus and Lenaeus, convinced him to flee after Antiochus had seized much of Egypt; they were possibly trying to undermine Ptolemy (cf. Ps 41:9). Ptolemy did so, but Antiochus captured him, and Ptolemy's little brother, Ptolemy VII,[29]

---

26. "There had been no reason to regard the exiled Antiochus as a potential successor to his brother Seleucus IV," (Goldingay, *Daniel*, 299).

27. Ibid., 300.

28. "To the pious Jews, the priesthood was of divine origin, but to Antiochus IV Epiphanes, the high priesthood was a mere political office," (Turner, *Daniel*, 243).

29. For the love of all that is Greek, can't we come up with a different name than "Ptolemy"? And how arrogant is it to give your name to two of your sons!?

became king (cf. 11:25–26). Antiochus attempted to control Egypt from afar by installing Ptolemy VI as a rival against Ptolemy VII (remember that both boys, as sons of Cleopatra, were Antiochus' nephews), but no sooner had Antiochus started for home than the two brothers buried the hatchet, deciding to rule jointly as co-regents over Egypt. I bet they wore obnoxious matching outfits, too. Meanwhile, Antiochus stopped to plunder the Jerusalem Temple on his way home because he was short of funds (cf. 11:28; 1 Macc 1:20–28; Josephus, Apion 2.84).

In 168, Antiochus IV attacked Egypt again, furious that his nephews had allied against him. Things didn't go so well for Antiochus this time since the brothers appealed to Rome for help. In what must have been an epic showdown, the Roman envoy Gaius Popillius Laenas confronted Antiochus at Alexandria and gave him an ultimatum to return home or face Rome's wrath. Antiochus hemmed and hawed, saying something like "I'll have to talk to my people and get back to you." But his stalling didn't work—Gaius drew a circle around Antiochus and ordered him not to step out until he had given Gaius an answer. Antiochus, embarrassed and angry, nonetheless capitulated (cf. 11:29–30; Polybius, *Histories* 29.27).

Somehow, a rumor began that Antiochus had died in Egypt. Hearing this, Jason launched an attack attempting to unseat Menelaus as the high priest. On his way home, Antiochus heard of the violence in Palestine and suspected a revolt was taking place. Still smarting over Rome having thrown down the gauntlet at Alexandria, he and his army came to Jerusalem and massacred 80,000 men, women, and children on the Sabbath (2 Macc 5:12–14). Antiochus also stationed troops in a citadel near the Temple (cf. Neh 2:8), an act of sacrilege in the minds of God's people.

But this wasn't the worst of it. Antiochus banned sacrifices and all Temple worship. Other religious observances so critical to the Law and Jewish identity (e.g. Sabbath, circumcision, kosher laws) were also prohibited. Torah scrolls were publicly burned. The worst of it came in December 167 when Antiochus "erected a desolating sacrilege on the altar of burnt offering" (1 Macc 1:54 NRSV). Specifically, he sacrificed a pig to Zeus on the holy altar (cf. 11:31).

There were varied responses to Antiochus' antics. Some, no doubt due to Antiochus' slick politics, went along with everything, turning their back on the Law of Moses and the covenant (1 Macc 2:18). But other Jews resisted (1 Macc 1:62–63), and some of those quite violently, eventually culminating in the Maccabean revolt. These were very difficult times for the faithful in Israel (cf. 11:32–35), as 1 Macc 1–2 and 2 Macc 6–7 bear out (see also Josephus, *Antiquities* 12.5.4–5). But notice how the divine messenger mentions "the wise" in 11:33, 35. He was referring to those Jews (perhaps the Hasidim, ancestors of the Pharisees) who knew the Scriptures and were faithful to the Lord. Unlike their unfaithful countrymen, they were spiritually equipped to face these difficult times because *they knew the Word and knew God*!

During this period, it is clear God allowed Antiochus to do almost whatever he wanted, but that included Antiochus adopting the moniker *Theou Epiphanes*, meaning "God manifest" or "God revealed." Beginning in 169, minted coins bore Antiochus' profile and this claim to divinity.[30] In many ways, Antiochus diverged from the policies and traditions of his predecessors. While the Seleucids had worshiped Apollo ("the gods of his fathers"), and the Ptolemies had patronized Adonis[31] ("the one beloved by women"), Antiochus promoted the Zeus cult (cf. 11:37–38). That Antiochus went way too far is seen in how his contemporaries secretly gave him an amended nickname, *Epimanes*, meaning "madman."[32] Despite his blasphemy, the true God of heaven would allow Antiochus to reign "till the indignation is accomplished," a haunting reminder that Antiochus was

30. Chisholm references 2 Macc 9:8 and how "Antiochus thought 'he could command the waves of the sea' and 'weigh the high mountains in a balance,' as if he were the sovereign creator and king of the world," (*Handbook on the Prophets*, 322). "For him, as for other kings, religion was the servant of his political position. He *is* more important than any god," (Goldingay, *Daniel*, 304).

31. The same goddess worshipped as Tammuz by the women of Ezekiel's day (Ezek 8:14).

32. "What is particularly important for Daniel is not simply Antiochus' hubris, but the fact that it was directed 'against a God of gods', the God of Israel. Having provoked the wrath of God, his end is certain," (Lucas, *Daniel*, 289).

a scourge against Israel as discipline for her sins (cf. 11:36). But his reign was not indefinite; God always appoints an end to his people's suffering!

Up to 11:40, this chapter has been a striking prediction of what was yet to take place in Daniel's time. Since 11:21, the story has concerned the reign of Antiochus IV, but the final six verses of Dan 11 do not match anything from Antiochus' life,[33] though there seems to be no identifiable break in the subject of 11:21–39 and 11:40–45 (some argue the break should be recognized at 11:36). As discussed in chapter 8, we know from secular historians that Antiochus died while in Persia, and from a sudden illness, rather than in battle.

That's why some interpreters claim these final six verses point to an end-times Antichrist figure foreshadowed by Antiochus, known as the man of lawlessness in 2 Thess 2 and the beast of Rev 13. These interpreters connect this Antichrist figure in Dan 11 to the little horn of Dan 7; the three horns plucked up by the little horn (7:8, 20) are supposedly Egypt, Libya, and Ethiopia (11:42–43). But all of this seems a stretch; there is nothing in the text indicating we should skip ahead to the end of time to understand the passage.[34] Others, like Turner, consider 11:40–45 to be a general review of Antiochus' life,[35] but the phrase "At the time of the end" (11:40) seems to nix that argument.[36] Interpreters of yesteryear considered these verses to be about Herod the Great, the

33. "The expositors who apply these vv. to Antiochus are faced with grave difficulty," (Young, *Daniel*, 250). "As soon as the attempt is made consistently to apply these verses to the king last spoken of [i.e. Antiochus], the difficulties begin to become overwhelming," (Leupold, *Daniel*, 510).

34. Goldingay, *Daniel*, 305. For the record, I personally do not see any allusion to an end-times Antichrist figure in the book of Daniel. Nor am I interested in identifying such a person since many have made what proved to be a false identification. Instead, I am content to rest in the knowledge that, when Jesus appears, he will destroy all opposed to him (2 Thess 2:8; cf. Rev 19:15).

35. Turner, *Daniel*, 255.

36. Lucas, *Daniel*, 292.

Roman Empire,[37] the rise of Islam, or the Catholic papacy. During the height of the Cold War, it was popular to identify Russia with the king of the north, but as you can imagine, few buy into that idea anymore.[38]

In light of so much rampant speculation, we might be making things too hard on ourselves by taking the passage literally. There are several ties between 11:40–45 and the prophecies of Isaiah Ezekiel that predict the overthrow of Assyria and Babylon. "Maybe it [Dan 11:40–45] is not a detailed prediction about Antiochus's end, but a promise that that end will come, using the language of earlier prophets."[39] Put another way, the divine messenger may be predicting the demise of Antiochus using popular phrases and imagery from the prophets. If I said, "I'm gonna make you an offer you can't refuse," you wouldn't take me literally, but you'd have a fair idea of what I was getting at if you'd seen *The Godfather*. The same goes for phrases such as "We're not in Kansas anymore," "We'll always have Paris," or "Houston, we have a problem."

Regardless of who is being discussed in 11:40–45, we cannot miss the great climax of the passage—"he shall come to his end." No ruler, no matter how oppressive he might be, can stand against God forever. Every wicked king eventually feels the brunt of the derision of heaven.[40] As we have seen before, a detailed account of things to come should not be used to help us guess what happens next, but to deepen our faith in the greatness and faithfulness of God. He is in control, he will keep his promises, and he will never forsake, but will rather be with us until the end (Matt 28:20).

37. So Hailey, but he also freely admits, "Any position that one seeks to defend presents problems," (*Daniel*, 232–40).

38. Carl Armerding, "Russia and the King of the North," *BibSac* 120 (1963): 50–55; J. Paul Tanner, "Daniel's "King of the North": Do We Owe Russia an Apology?" *JETS* 35 (1992): 315–28.

39. Ernest C. Lucas, "Book of Daniel" in *Dictionary for Theological Interpretation of the Bible*, ed., Kevin J. Vanhoozer (Grand Rapids: Baker, 2005), 159.

40. "Despite the fact that rulers become strong, suddenly they stand no longer; their kingdoms are broken, they retreat, they fall. This pattern recurs in the remainder of the chapter and emphasizes the fleeting glory achieved by conquest," (Baldwin, *Daniel*, 189).

As more time passes, the promise of God's presence becomes sweeter to his saints. Praise God for never abandoning his people!

## DANIEL 12

Appropriately, the book of Daniel ends somewhat enigmatically. The beginning of Dan 12 mentions the rise of the archangel Michael, mixed with a very turbulent period "such as never has been." But Daniel is assured his people, particularly those whose names are in the book of life, will be delivered. The resurrected will shine like stars. Daniel is then told to seal the book until "the time of the end." There is also the cryptic phrase, "Many shall run to and fro, and knowledge shall increase" (12:4).

These verses do not have to do with the end of time, but nor do they refer to the period of Antiochus. Remember that the vision of Dan 10–12 concerned Daniel's people, i.e. Israel. It thus seems as if Dan 12 refers somewhat to Rome's destruction of Jerusalem in A.D. 70, but also to how God delivered his faithful people in the midst of such a difficult period. Jesus described these events as a "great tribulation, such as has not been from the beginning of the world until now, no, and never will be" (Matt 24:21). If Jesus alluded to Dan 12 in Matt 24, how can these verses have to do exclusively with the time of Antiochus?

During the Maccabean revolt, it was commonly believed that the Jews received divine aid in battle (2 Macc 10:29–30; 11:6–13; 15:22–27). Whether the archangel Michael gave direct help to God's people then is uncertain, but it's not a stretch to believe that he protected the church at God's direction when Rome came against Jerusalem. As we discovered in the previous chapter, Christians abandoned Jerusalem because they remembered Jesus' warning. Rome's wrath only affected those Jews who had rejected Jesus as the Messiah. We must thus adopt a new definition of "God's people." In light of the gospel, it is no longer limited to descendants of Israel, but to all those who are in Christ (Gal 3:28). Just as John the Baptist denied any special significance in being a physical descendant of Abraham (Matt 3:9–10), so also Paul chastised those Jews who identified with the covenant people outwardly, but not inwardly (Rom 2:28–29).

Is the resurrection mentioned in 12:2 the final, bodily resurrection set to occur when Jesus returns? Or is it a spiritual resurrection experienced in the gospel? Scholars are divided on the issue, and I believe the evidence in this passage is inconclusive. Jesus spoke of the final resurrection using similar language (John 5:28–29), but a few verses earlier, seemed to allude to a spiritual resurrection (John 5:24; cf. Rom 6:5; Eph 2:5).[41] It may not matter which resurrection is in view in Dan 12 since those who are resurrected spiritually with Christ in baptism (Rom 6:3–6) indeed have the hope of everlasting life where they will shine like stars (12:2–3; cf. 1 Cor 15:41–42; 2 Tim 4:8).

The command to "shut up the words and seal the book" meant Daniel was to make sure its message was safeguarded. To "seal" a scroll meant to place one's signet ring in hot wax over the scroll's closing as a mark of authenticity. The scroll was then placed in a secure location. Whenever important documents (e.g. legal or financial) were sealed and "shut up" in ancient times, it was to protect the original copy should there ever be a dispute as to its contents[42] (cf. Jer 32:11, 14). Remember that, when Daniel received this vision, Cyrus had only been reigning a few years, and the events described in Dan 11 were several centuries in the future. It's no wonder Daniel could not understand these things (12:8).[43] But by sealing it's contents and placing it in a safe place, Daniel's prophetic word could be retrieved as these things came to pass; his claims would be validated, and the people of God would be inspired to continue trusting in the only One who knows the end from the beginning.

---

41. There's a chance that 12:2 was fulfilled by the very odd scene in Matt 27:52 –53, but as Coffman (*Daniel*, 184) notes, this only mentions the resurrection of the righteous, not the wicked, and not even these were raised to everlasting life.

42. Archer, "Daniel," 153–54.

43. "If the prophet himself heard and did not understand, what will be the case with those men who presumptuously expound a book which has been sealed, and that too unto the time of the end, a book which is shrouded with many obscurities?" (Jerome, *Daniel*, 150).

In contrast to these saints who sought understanding and encouragement in the Word of God (cf. Rom 15:4), Daniel is told, "Many shall run to and fro, and knowledge shall increase." This statement is very similar to Amos 8:11–12. In troubled times, whether centuries ago, or in centuries to come, there will be those who seek signs and messages from the Lord, all the while refusing to read what God has so clearly said in Scripture.[44]

At this point, Daniel noticed two angels on opposite banks of the Tigris, and one of them asked the mysterious "man" of Dan 10, "How long will it be before these astonishing things are fulfilled?" (12:6 NIV; cf. 1 Pet 1:12). The "man" solemnly swore by God himself (cf. Gen 14:22; Exod 6:8; Deut 32:40; Ezek 20:5; Rev 10:5–6)[45] that the period would last an ambiguous "time, times, and half a time" (12:7; cf. 7:25). We're given a little more of an idea of when this period would end by the phrase "the shattering of the power of the holy people," i.e. the time when the Jews' power would be broken by Rome's destruction of Jerusalem. This terrible event was punishment for the Jews having rejected Jesus, so the Son of Man dashed "them in pieces like a potter's vessel" (cf. Ps 2:9–12). When Daniel inquired further, he was told to go his way, i.e. to continue living his life.[46]

The divine messenger tells Daniel that 1,290 days would pass between the suspension of Temple worship and the end of the period. But then comes another confusing statement—"Blessed is he who waits and arrives at the 1,335 days" (12:12). Lucas says, "No-one has been able to suggest a satisfactory explanation of the two time periods given in vv. 11–12. ... Whatever the actual meaning of the numbers, the significance

44. "The written revelation of God is in the world, but men heed it not. Instead, they look for knowledge where it is not to be found," (Young, *Daniel*, 258).

45. "The raising of *both* hands by the man dressed in linen must signify a particularly solemn oath," (Lucas, *Daniel*, 297).

46. "So he is bidden back to the common paths of life, and is enjoined to pursue his patient course with an eye on the end to which it conducts, and to leave the unknown future to unfold itself as it may," (Maclaren, *Expositions*, 84).

of them is as an encouragement to perseverance because the suffering has a time limit and will end fairly soon."[47] Symbolic or otherwise, the phrase likely has to do with the destruction of Jerusalem. From the time the Romans first appeared at Jerusalem to the final sacrifice being offered in the Temple was about 3½ years. The additional 45 days may be a way of saying, "Soon after the final sacrifice, the period of oppression will be brought to an end. Hold on a little while longer!"

Or, to use Jesus' words, "the one who endures to the end will be saved" (Matt 24:13).

47. Lucas, *Daniel*, 297–98; cf. Baldwin, *Daniel*, 210.

## TALKING POINTS

SCRIPTURE IS CLEAR that God's people are engaged in war. "Because we live in a physical world, we sometimes forget that we are also spiritual beings. A person who is in touch with only the physical is simply not facing all that is real."[48] Even in our struggles against ungodly family members, hostile neighbors, and arrogant superiors, much is at stake spiritually. So how are we to engage in spiritual warfare? From a survey of NT teaching, it seems our primary weapons include prayer, evangelism, and good works. In prayer, we not only align our priorities with God's, but we also lend a mysterious hand to the angels fighting on our behalf.[49] Prayer becomes a rather formidable weapon when we petition for our enemies to repent and be forgiven. But active evangelism is also a formidable weapon at our disposal; when the 72 sent out by Jesus returned, he said he had seen Satan fall from heaven during their endeavors (Luke 10:18). Finally, good works are a weapon since we thereby heap metaphorical coals on the heads of our enemies (Rom 12:21). According to Peter, good works are one of only two acceptable responses to oppression (1 Pet 4:19). We are to reject carnal, sinful weapons and lay claim instead to divine power. Satan and his demons tremble in unmitigated fear when the church wages war in a way that honors God; they know their schemes are of no effect against us (2 Cor 10:3–4). In the dark days that lie ahead, let us resolve to fight God's way, not the world's way.

THERE ARE TIMES when, quite frankly, it will seem the events of history have no clear direction or purpose. One nation rises and another

48. Myers, *Daniel*, 358.

49. "After all is said on this difficult chapter, we should not lose sight of the fact that its whole function was to encourage Daniel to faithfulness in prayer. By showing him that the real conflict lying behind world events is spiritual (cf. chapter 10), the Lord was teaching Daniel that the real weapon of the church is prayer. Fail in the work of prayer, and we fail to understand this great vision," (Ferguson, *Daniel*, 239–40).

falls; one tyrant holds power for a lifetime, while another is deposed after just a few days. But this chapter makes clear that God is in control, even in the most random of circumstances.[50] Remarkably, no one king in Dan 11 successfully holds power for very long, not even Antiochus. The most ambitious and tyrannical of rulers is still held in check by God. Christians know "the rest of the story." Not every detail leading up to the end has been revealed to us, but we have been assured of the final outcome. That's why we can read tomorrow's news with all the tranquility of a sleeping child in its mother's arms. Christians don't know what the future holds, but we know who holds the future. Let us, therefore, confess with Paul: "I know whom I have believed, and am convinced that he is able to guard what I have entrusted to him until that day" (2 Tim 1:12 NIV).

FINALLY, THE ENTIRETY of Daniel's experiences with God's revealed word reminds us of our own enormous burden. Prayer and Bible study are not activities to be taken lightly, but are to be entered into with much fear and trembling; "it is no light thing to receive God's 'word'" (Jer 20:9).[51] These endeavors should cost us something! Lengthy study led Daniel to humble himself and pour his heart out in prayer, seeking understanding. Prayer sometimes led to mysterious visions, and these visions affected him physically in a significant way—it's possible he often felt as if he had received more than he bargained for! Our faith won't survive coming days of trouble unless these spiritual disciplines weigh on us as they did on Daniel. This is of particular relevance to those who regularly minister the Word to God's people. We will never be any better than peddlers of cotton candy preaching if we only search the Scriptures (or worse, "some new thing" from fallible mortals) for our next lesson. The church will always need bold and faithful leadership. If we are to fill such roles, let us not only commit ourselves to God's unmerited blessing, but also to the disciplines

50. Wallace, *The Lord Is King*, 188.

51. Russell, *Daniel*, 194.

of prayer and Bible study. In so doing, we will be ushered before God's throne, compelled to kneel in awe-struck wonder, and humbly convicted of our weaknesses. Only then are we equipped for the King's service.

# ABBREVIATIONS

| | |
|---|---|
| ANE | Ancient Near East(ern) |
| *AUSS* | *Andrews University Seminary Studies* |
| *BAR* | *Biblical Archaeology Review* |
| *BibSac* | *Bibliotheca Sacra* |
| *CBQ* | *Catholic Biblical Quarterly* |
| DBI | *Dictionary of Biblical Imagery*. Ed. Leland Ryken, James C. Wilhoit, and Tremper Longman III. Downers Grove, IL: InterVarsity Press, 1998. |
| ESV | English Standard Version |
| HALOT | *The Hebrew and Aramaic Lexicon of the Old Testament*. Ludwig Koehler, Walter Baumgartner. Trans. and ed. M. E. J. Richardson. 5 vols. Leiden: Brill, 1994–2000. |
| HCSB | Holman Christian Standard Bible |
| *JBL* | *Journal of Biblical Literature* |
| *JETS* | *Journal of the Evangelical Theological Society* |
| *JSJ* | *Journal for the Study of Judaism* |
| *JSOT* | *Journal for the Study of the Old Testament* |
| KJV | King James Version |

| | |
|---|---|
| LXX | Septuagint, the Greek translation of the Old Testament |
| Msg | The Message |
| NASU | New American Standard Bible — Updated Edition |
| NCV | New Century Version |
| NIDOTTE | *New International Dictionary of Old Testament Theology and Exegesis.* Ed. Willem A. VanGemeren. 5 vols. Grand Rapids: Zondervan, 1997. |
| NIV | New International Version |
| NLT | New Living Translation |
| NRSV | New Revised Standard Version |
| NT | New Testament |
| OT | Old Testament |
| *RevQ* | *Revue de Qumran* |
| *Them* | *Themelios* |
| *TynBul* | *Tyndale Bulletin* |
| *VT* | *Vetus Testamentum* |
| *WTJ* | *Westminster Theological Journal* |

# ACKNOWLEDGMENTS

To my Keurig and the coffee it dispenses—"Oh, my dear friend! You're so beautiful!" (Songs 1:15 Msg).

To my church family in Bowie. I appreciate your forbearance as I preached through this material. Your support of my writing endeavors has been a great encouragement to me. I also want to acknowledge those friends who prayed faithfully for me during the writing of this book. God knows who you are, and be assured I love each of you with all my heart.

To Billy Alexander for allowing me to borrow his books.

To Bill Camp, Jimmy Gee, Dale Jenkins, Jeff Jenkins, Rusty Pettus, Paul Reid, and Stephen Sutton for believing in this project and supporting it so generously.

To Jordan and Shelly Mullins. Everyone should be blessed to have such great friends as you.

To Shirley Eaton. Your assistance has been invaluable. Thanks for being generous in so many ways.

To Pam Ashley, Sheri Glazier, Josh James, and Rebecca Thompson for selfless editorial work. The only reason this book is readable is because of their diligence.

To Sam Dawson, Tim Gunnells, and LaGard Smith for reviewing the manuscript and offering input.

To LaGard Smith for writing such an extraordinary *Foreword*.

To Daniel Isaac. Never forget these three things, my son: I love you. Fear not the beast. Kiss the Son.

To Skippy DIL. You're every line. You're every word. You're everything.

To the God of Daniel, Hananiah, Mishael, and Azariah. "To him who sits on the throne and to the Lamb be blessing and honor and glory and might forever and ever!" (Rev 5:13).

# BIBLIOGRAPHY


Anderson, Robert A. *Signs and Wonders*. Grand Rapids: Eerdmans, 1984.

Archer, Gleason L., Jr. "Daniel" in *The Expositor's Bible Commentary*. Vol. 7. Grand Rapids: Zondervan, 1985.

Baldwin, Joyce G. *Daniel*. Downers Grove, IL: InterVarsity Press, 1978.

Boice, James Montgomery. *Daniel*. Grand Rapids: Zondervan, 1989.

Calvin, John. *Commentaries on the Book of the Prophet Daniel*. 2 vols. Trans. Thomas Myers. Grand Rapids: Eerdmans, 1948.

Chisholm, Robert B., Jr. *Handbook on the Prophets*. Grand Rapids: Baker, 2002.

Coffman, James Burton. *Commentary on Daniel*. Abilene, TX: ACU Press, 1989.

Collins, John J. *Daniel*. Minneapolis: Fortress, 1993.

Ferguson, Sinclair B. *Daniel*. Waco: Word, 1988.

Fewell, Danna Nolan. *Circle of Sovereignty*. 2nd ed. Nashville: Abingdon, 1991.

Ginzberg, Louis. *The Legends of the Jews*. Vol. 4. Philadelphia: Jewish Publication Society, 1968.

Goldingay, John E. *Daniel*. Dallas: Word, 1989.

Hailey, Homer. *A Commentary on Daniel*. Las Vegas: Nevada Publications, 2001.

Hill, Andrew E. "Daniel" in *The Expositor's Bible Commentary*. Rev. ed. Vol. 8. Grand Rapids: Zondervan, 2008.

Ironside, H. A. *Lectures on Daniel the Prophet*. 2nd ed. Neptune, NJ: Loizeaux, 1920.

Jamieson, Robert, A. R. Fausset, and David Brown. *A Commentary Critical, Experimental and Practical on the Old and New Testament*. Vol. 4. Grand Rapids: Eerdmans, 1948.

Jerome. *Commentary on Daniel*. Trans. Gleason L. Archer, Jr. Grand Rapids: Baker, 1958.

Keil, C. F. *Biblical Commentary on the Book of Daniel*. Trans. M. G. Easton. Grand Rapids: Eerdmans, 1949.

Koldewey, Robert. *The Excavations of Babylon*. Trans. Agnes S. Johns. London: Macmillan, 1914.

Leupold, H. C. *Exposition of Daniel*. Grand Rapids: Baker, 1949.

Lacocque, André. *The Book of Daniel*. Trans. David Pellauer. Atlanta: John Knox, 1979.

Lewis, Jack P. *The Major Prophets*. Henderson, TN: Hester Publications, 1999.

Longman, Tremper, III. *Daniel*. Grand Rapids: Zondervan, 1999.

—. *Reading the Bible with Heart and Mind*. Colorado Springs: NavPress, 1997.

Lucas, Ernest C. *Daniel*. Downers Grove, IL: InterVarsity Press, 2002.

Maclaren, Alexander. *Expositions of Holy Scripture: Ezekiel, Daniel, and the Minor Prophets*. Grand Rapids: Eerdmans, 1938.

McGuiggan, Jim. *The Book of Daniel*. Lubbock, TX: Sunset Institute Press, 2011.

Miller, Stephen R. *Daniel*. Nashville: Broadman, 1994.

Montgomery, James A. *A Critical and Exegetical Commentary on the Book of Daniel*. Edinburgh: T & T Clark, 1927.

Myers, Edward P., Neale T. Pryor, and David R. Rechtin. *Daniel*. Searcy, AR: Resource Publications, 2012.

Oppenheim, A. Leo. *Ancient Mesopotamia*. Rev. ed. Chicago: Univ. of Chicago Press, 1977.

Russell, D. S. *Daniel*. Philadelphia: Westminster Press, 1981.

Schaeffer, Francis A. *No Little People*. Downers Grove, IL: InterVarsity Press, 1974.

Turner, Rex A., Sr. *Daniel*. Montgomery: Southern Christian Univ., 1993.

Wallace, Ronald S. *The Lord Is King*. Downers Grove, IL: InterVarsity Press, 1979.

Wiersbe, Warren W. *Be Resolute*. Colorado Springs: Victor, 2000.

Wiseman, D. J. *Nebuchadrezzar and Babylon*. Oxford: Oxford Univ. Press, 1985.

Wood, Leon. *A Commentary on Daniel*. Grand Rapids: Zondervan, 1973.

Young, Edward J. *The Prophecy of Daniel*. Grand Rapids: Eerdmans, 1949.

ὥσπερ ξένοι χαίρουσι πατρίδα βλέπειν
οὕτως καὶ τοῖς κάμνουσι βιβλίου τέλος

CPSIA information can be obtained
at www.ICGtesting.com
Printed in the USA
FFOW04n1012071114
8535FF